Daniel D. Barnard

The Sovereignty of the States Over Their Navigable Waters:

Argument of Daniel D. Barnard, in the Albany Bridge Case, Submitted to the Supreme Court of the United States, at the Term Held in the City of Washington, in February, 1860

Daniel D. Barnard

The Sovereignty of the States Over Their Navigable Waters:
Argument of Daniel D. Barnard, in the Albany Bridge Case, Submitted to the Supreme Court of the United States, at the Term Held in the City of Washington, in February, 1860

ISBN/EAN: 9783337818081

Printed in Europe, USA, Canada, Australia, Japan

Cover: Foto ©ninafisch / pixelio.de

More available books at **www.hansebooks.com**

THE SOVEREIGNTY OF THE STATES OVER THEIR NAVIGABLE WATERS.

ARGUMENT

OF

DANIEL D. BARNARD,

IN THE

ALBANY BRIDGE CASE,

SUBMITTED TO THE

Supreme Court of the United States,

AT THE TERM HELD IN THE

CITY OF WASHINGTON,

IN FEBRUARY, 1860.

———••———

ALBANY:
ATLAS & ARGUS PRINT.
1860.

IN THE
SUPREME COURT
OF THE
UNITED STATES,
IN EQUITY.

ROBERT D. SILLIMAN, *vs.* THE HUDSON RIVER BRIDGE CO.	
FREDERICK W. COLEMAN, *vs.* THE SAME.	

ARGUMENT OF D. D. BARNARD FOR DEFENDANT.

I.

This case comes before the Court in a way to involve questions of a good deal of magnitude and interest; one of which, at least, and that the highest of all in importance, has never, so far as I know, received the deliberate consideration of this Court.

The particular question referred to, has relation to the extent to which the authority of Congress, under the power " to regulate commerce," may be carried in asserting a supremacy of sovereignty and jurisdiction in the Government of the United States, both on the waters and on the land, within the territorial limits of the several States, over the sovereignty and jurisdiction of the States. To that question I shall ask leave to call the special attention of the Court before concluding my argument.

This case arises from the action of the Legislature of the State of New York—the supreme power in the State—taken to establish a bridge across the Hudson River at Albany. The Act for this object was passed in 1856, and a supplementary Act in 1857. The State proceeds by a mode usual in the States in prosecuting their works of public improvement—by incorporating a Company with authority to erect a bridge, under the special limitations and instructions of the Act of Incorporation.

The State of New York, as everybody knows, beginning early, has accomplished a good deal in the way of public improvements. Having the Bay of New York, with the commercial emporium of the country seated upon its shores, and having the Hudson River ascending from it, and navigable for vessels and steamers of large size for 150 miles—a great highway of commerce—she early adopted, and has executed, plans by which she has extended this water highway, by a grand system of artificial rivers, through her entire territory, north and west; and has thus brought her great river and bay, opening to the sea, and her great commercial city, through a thoroughfare of navigable waters, into a direct commercial connection with a foreign country of vast extent on her northern boundary, and a chain and system of States of the Union, actual and prospective, in the boundless West—where still "the star of empire" seems to take its way.

Already the connected commerce on these navigable waters of the State, natural and artificial, is immense. With the completion of the enlargement of the canals, it cannot fail to be greatly increased. As a valuable portion of that which passes on the Hudson, in connection with the canals, employs the river above Albany, it is the highest interest of the State to take care that the navigation of the river at and above Albany, as well as below, shall be preserved.

But the State has highways of commerce on the land as well as on the water. Besides its common roads and turnpikes, it has an immense system of railways, stretching through the State by various routes, constructed at vast cost, and bearing vast amounts of commerce and travel. The great central line of this system of railways connects New York with Buffalo, and the almost limitless West, and crosses the river at Albany. Other lines, one coming westward from Boston, and another coming southward from Canada, and the States north and east, also cross the river at Albany.

Ferries have been established at Albany from the earliest time, and always maintained under colonial and State authority. At the present time, besides two steam ferry-boats for common use, and kept in almost constant motion, there are two others which have thus far served, very imperfectly of course, to supply the broken link in the otherwise continuous lines of railway just referred to. Nearly 4,000 passengers cross the river daily in connection with these railways—a good deal more than a million a year, and more than 500,000 tons of freight. Ferry-boats afford very inadequate and inconvenient means for a business of such magnitude.

The State finally concluded, in 1856, that the time had come—the population of the State having run up to a sum greater than that of the whole Union at the Revolution, and the movement of property and persons on her highways of commerce, being much greater than in ordinary proportion to the population—when better facilities ought to be afforded, and were, in her judgment, imperatively demanded, for so much of this movement of property and persons as must traverse the Hudson at Albany.

She determined, therefore, to establish a bridge at this point. She believed that a bridge could be so constructed that while it would afford increased facilities for the traverse of the river, it would still leave the navigation of the river free for all useful purposes, with no other inconveniences than such partial ones as must always arise, to some extent, in works of this character, and which, by the very necessities of the law of general improvement and progress, must be submitted to, in consideration of the just accommodation required to be afforded to other public interests, quite as important as those to which such partial inconveniences may apply, and equally entitled to the fostering care and protection of the government.

The State was the proper guardian of both interests, and of all interests affected by the measure, certainly to the extent to which the domestic commerce and travel of the State were concerned. It acted for both interests; and for both interests in that ampler view which embraces so much of the foreign commerce of the country, and of the commerce between the States, as moves upon, or traverses the river at this point, and in the protection and preservation of which the State of New York has a deeper stake, certainly than any other State, and than a good many States combined.

It is not an unimportant consideration in this connection, that the immense interests involved in the Postal and Military systems of the United States, coming within the State of New York, do naturally, and must of moral necessity, seek and employ the same channels of communication, and the same means and facilities, artificial as well as natural, for traversing the State, as the commerce of the State employs.

I think it may be said, without fear of gain-saying, that if the Government of the United States had undertaken to make post-roads and military roads for itself in the State of New York, and if it had gone further, and undertaken a grand system of internal improvements in this State by making roads, canals and railways, for promoting and facilitating that foreign commerce, and commerce between the States, which it is its province to "regulate," it could not have devised a system of improvements more perfectly fitted to all such national uses, than that which has been prepared by the State alone, under its original and undoubted power to make roads, canals, railways and bridges, not in conflict with the Constitution of the United States or any law of Congress, for the benefit of the domestic interests of the State, and of the commerce belonging to or passing through it.

The State has believed that its system of public improvements was very incomplete without the addition of a bridge at Albany. And if the State had not embarked in this enterprise, and if the Government of the United States was competent to undertake it, and could have done so with propriety under any power it possesses, I think Congress could scarcely have done anything, on the same scale, of greater usefulness, or of more pressing importance, for the national objects under its charge within the State of New York— for its post system and mails, for military uses, and for whatever might facilitate foreign and inter-State commerce in this quarter of the Union—than itself to construct just such a bridge at Albany as the State now proposes to establish.

This Court will not presume, nor be lightly convinced, that the State has entered on this enterprise without due consideration of all the interests that may be affected by it. Nor will it assume, or be easily persuaded, that it is itself a better judge than the State can be, however enlightened by any testimony which interested parties may bring before it, of the various questions, physical and economical, involved in it. These same parties, be it remembered, and all parties opposed to the measure, as well as those in its favor, have been heard, with whatever testimony they chose to offer, before appropriate committees of the Legislature, before the enterprise was adopted.

Now the Court has the authoritative and formal announcement in the Acts of the Legislature of New York authorizing the bridge, and which I know it will take pleasure in treating with all respect, that the State believes that a necessity had arisen for a bridge over the Hudson at Albany; that the time had come when it was its duty to provide for the transit over the river, by that means, of the great and growing press of commerce and travel seeking passage at that point; and that a bridge could be constructed under the directions, limitations and provisions of the Act of the Legislature, which would not obstruct, or materially impede or injure the accustomed use of the river for navigation at and above the bridge, or occasion any material loss or damage to individual property, or to the business interests of any locality or community whatever.

Can this Court, under any conceivable circumstances, be a better judge of these grave matters than the State, to which they would seem more appropriately to belong? Is it a proper exercise of judicial power in this Court—is it the exercise of a judicial power at all—for this Court to sit as a Council of Revision over the Acts of a State Legislature on such questions as these — questions fit only for legislative investigation and decision; when the only ground on which the Court can be asked to entertain them in the present stage of the business is, that at the end of its investigations, and its examination of 5,650 legal folios — more than one thousand octavo pages of closely printed matter — in the form of evidence, almost wholly speculative in character, it might reach a conclusion different from that at which the State had arrived in regard to the necessity, the general propriety, and the safety to the public interests, of a bridge at Albany.

This case first came to a hearing before his Honor Mr. Justice Nelson, in the autumn of 1856, upon a motion for a Preliminary Injunction. On this motion, in July 1857, the State was laid under a Judicial Interdict in regard to the establishing of a bridge, as authorized and provided for in the Act of the Legislature, and has so remained now for two years and a half.

And this Interdict was laid, not because the Court had come to a conclusion, upon the proofs then before it, adverse to the right of the State to construct such a bridge as was proposed; not because the Court was of opinion that the State had misjudged in its estimate of the effect to be produceed by the bridge upon the navigation of the river; not because the Court was of opinion that the State had passed a law for this object which was in conflict with the Constitution, or any law of Congress; not because the party complaining had made out any case whatever against the sovereign right of the State in the premises; but because the Court, at some future day, and on further proofs, might be brought to conclude that the State had so far erred on the purely speculative question of the effect to be produced on the navigation, as that a conflict between the State law and some law of Congress might arise, or manifest itself, if the bridge should be established.

The mischiefs of this early, and, as it will be my duty to insist in this argument, entirely premature interposition of the Court in a case of this sort, are apparent in this very proceeding.

His honor, Mr. Justice Nelson, for whom I beg to say I entertain the highest respect, in the opinion delivered by him, on granting the Preliminary Injunction, declared that, "in his judgment, the real and turning point in the case is, whether, or not, * * * the draw or draws will furnish reasonable means to prevent any substantial obstruction to the navigation." On this question, which, in the hands of the Court, must be one of pure speculation, the Court doubts, and upon this doubt the State is laid under interdict, and yet, all the while, it was an admitted fact in the case, that for three or more months in the year—always the most difficult and dangerous for the passage across the river—the navigation of the river is wholly closed by ice, during which the use of the bridge would be exceedingly important to the great interests intended to be secured by it, even if not allowed to use it at all for the rest of the year, and when, of course, no possible question of obstruction by the closing of the draw or draws, could arise.

I shall endeavor, by and by, to satisfy this Court that in any case where a question of conflict is made between a law of a State passed under an admitted power, and a law of Congress passed under another and a different power, and where no question of conflict arises on the face, or by the terms of the State law, it is quite time enough for the jurisdiction of the Courts of the United States to be brought to bear upon the case, when some actual conflict or collision takes place by some act, or the exercise of some authority, under the State law, of such a character as may authorize and lead the Court to pronounce that the two laws cannot stand together, and each have a reasonable and fair execution and operation, but that one must give way. That of course must be the State law, since the Act of Congress must have the supremacy which the Constitution assigns to it.

This case having been again heard, upon further proofs, before the Circuit Court, and the two judges sitting at that Circuit having divided in opinion, the case comes before this Court for final adjudication.

II.

The case before the Court is this:

An Act had been passed by the Legislature of New York, authorising the erection of a bridge over the Hudson River at Albany.

Before anything was done towards the actual erection of the bridge, this suit was brought.

The parties complaining are : first, a citizen of Troy, and next, a citizen of Massachusetts.

Both claim rights to the free navigation of the Hudson River, under a license from the authorities of the United States, for the coasting trade.

The suit in form, is against a Chartered Company, which is authorized to construct the bridge. In substance and effect, it is against the State of New York. It is the State that has undertaken to establish a Bridge over the Hudson at Albany, for the public benefit, and as a part of its system of public improvements. It has proposed to do this through the very usual and accustomed agency of an Incorporated Company.

The matter complained of in the case, is a public law of the State, authorising the erection of a bridge, when, according to the complainants, no such bridge can be erected without violating rights secured to them by a paramount law of Congress.

It is thus that the complainants make a judicial case for themselves before the Court. They claim personal rights under an Act of Congress—the Act passed for granting licenses to vessels for the coasting trade. Having possessed themselves of such a license, for vessels owned by them respectively, and being accustomed to pursue the coasting trade, under that license, on the Hudson River, as far as Troy, where a port of delivery is established by law, they claim the right of free navigation to that point, and they complain that the law of the State authorising a bridge at Albany, will, if carried into execution, result in obstructing that free navigation, to their personal injury.

But the complainants in their Bills, set forth other grievances besides their own, and they arraign the State of New York before this Court, upon grave charges of error, and of faults worse than error, in the measure under consideration. They declare that the enterprise has been entered upon without any public necessity for it; that the public interests are well enough, and fully, subserved by existing facilities, without this bridge; that the State by this measure is sacrificing, or greatly injuring its own vast property and interests in the Erie and Champlain Canals; that individual property, real and personal, will be greatly and irretrievably impaired by it; and that the great manufacturing and other business interests, and property of the city of Troy, with its population of 40,000, and of the neighboring villages of West Troy and Green Island, with their population of 7,000 more, are about to receive great and irremediable injury at the hands of the State by this measure.

This rather serious arraignment of the State of New York before this Court, first by a citizen of Troy, and next by a citizen of Barnstable, in Massachusetts, discloses clearly enough who the real party in interest is, in this suit. The city of Troy does in this matter what she deems it for her interest to do, and nobody blames her for it. If she is more frightened than harmed, that is not an uncommon case. But, at least, we must not turn away our eyes from seeing that it is not so much the great public interests involved in the free navigation of the Hudson River which are represented by the nominal parties to this suit—in connection of course with the personal stake they have in the matter—as it is the alarms, if these are really felt, or the commendable aspirations and ambition of a particular community within the State of New York, numbering 40,000 out of the 3,500,000 of population, which the State has under its care and protection—a community which happens to have fixed the site of its beautiful domain a little too high up the river to catch all the advantages of commercial prosperity, and a little above the point where the State has thought that the public interests at large demanded that a bridge should be established.

Now I must take leave to say that the economical policy of the State in prosecuting this work of public improvement, and the effect that may be produced incidentally upon individual property, real or personal, or upon the general business interests of any particular city or community in the State, are not subjects fit to be presented to the consideration of the Court in this case, either with a view to invoke its condemnation of the policy of the State in this regard, or with a view to any influence such considerations might have upon the mind of the Court in deciding the proper and only judicial case before it.

No person could maintain an action in a Court of the State solely on the ground that the value of his property was deteriorated, or his general business interests injured, by any bridge, of any sort or description, which the State might authorize over the Hudson at Albany, so long as its authority over the subject as a sovereign power was not brought into question. Such general and incidental injuries to individual property, or to the business affairs of a particular locality, from the action of the State, in a work of public improvement, cannot have redress at the hands of the judiciary of the State. The redress, if any is to be had, or ought to be had, can come only from the legislative authority, upon the petition of the parties aggrieved.

If this bridge had been erected, and an action at law was brought on the ground of a claim of personal right to the free navigation of the river under a paramount law of Congress, the State Court might maintain that right. The action being at law, the recovery would be of damages in the particular interest secured to the plaintiff under the law of Congress, and nothing more. The action would be confined to the injury accruing from the interruption of his personal right to navigate the river. Injuries to property and interests which are in no way under the special protection of the general government, but remain under the guardianship of State laws, could not be made the ground of an action.

No suit in Equity for an Injunction to prevent the erection of a bridge, could be maintained in a State Court at all. No State Court would sit to hear an application for an Injunction by a private party, against the State, or against its agents created to carry into effect a measure of public improvement, on the allegation that the act of the Legislature was in conflict with a paramount law of Congress, unless the alleged conflict was apparent on the face of the Act, or was clearly inevitable if the proposed measure should be carried into effect. It would refuse to lay its hand upon the State, or its constituted agents, in the way of judicial interdict, as an unauthorized, and unseemly exercise of judicial authority. It could exercise such an authority on no other ground than that the State was about to commit a public nuisance, against the United States, by placing, or authorizing, an encroachment or obstruction to navigation, upon its own soil and property in the Hudson River, while, as yet, nothing appeared to impeach the perfect authority and validity of the law of the Legislature, but an allegation that a conflict between that law and some act of Congress, not apparent or inevitable, from the face and terms of the law, might arise hereafter, if the measure of the State should be prosecuted to completion.

This Court, I suppose, can exercise no other or larger jurisdiction in this case than a State Court could or would exercise if the same suit had been brought originally there, and the Court can have no rule of decision, in the absence, or beyond the scope, of Congressional legislation, but the law of the State.

This suit in Equity for an Injunction to prevent the proposed bridge being erected, can only be maintained on the ground that it would be a public nuisance against the United States. If it would not be that, the complainants certainly cannot maintain their suit for the private injury they set up as likely to arise from an interruption or impediment to their personal right to the free navigation of the river. The nuisance, if any, is to arise from an unlawful obstruction to the navigation of a public river. It will consist in this, and nothing else. It will be because the public of the United States, or at least such portion of the public as may, like the complainants, be armed with a supposed special authority from the general government to navigate the river, will be interrupted, or unlawfully impeded, in the use and enjoyment of this common right. It will not be a public nuisance against the United States, of which this Court can take notice, because the property or business interests of individual citizens of the State, or of any number of them, or of any particular community in the State, may be, or will be, injuriously affected as incident to the unlawful obstruction of the navigation of the river.

If then this Court, consenting to entertain this case on a Bill in Equity, (which I shall insist it ought not to do) should be of opinion that the proposed bridge, if erected, would be an unlawful obstruction to the free navigation of the river, as secured or guaranteed to the public, or a portion of the public, by the legislation of Congress, and therefore a public nuisance and offence against the United States, the Court, of course, if it thinks it has the power, will so decide. But the Court cannot be legitimately aided in reaching that conclusion by receiving suggestions, or proofs, to convince it, that the public policy of the State in this measure, as a State policy, was wrong, and that instead of benefitting, it would inflict injury on its own interests and its own people, unless its hand was stayed by the authority of this Court. Much less can the Court go beyond the jurisdiction which the legislation of Congress may be found to give it, in regard to the alleged public nuisance, to find a substantive ground of judicial action in any injuries charged, or likely to arise to the complainants, or to other citizens of the State of New York, in their property or interests, as incident to the erection of the proposed bridge, and not arising from any direct violation of their rights of free navigation.

Quite the contrary of all this. The courtesy due to a State requires the Court, (so I presume it will think,) to assume that the State has acted wisely in this measure in respect to the proper interests of the State, and of its own people; that there is, as the Act of the State indicates, a strong necessity for a bridge at Albany—a necessity for which the State was bound to provide, if it could, in the way proposed; that the bridge would be of great and general benefit to the people of the State, and all others having occasion to use it; and that if incidental loss or damage should accrue from the measure to any, few or many, in respect to their private property or their general business affairs, the justice of the State may be relied on, with sure confidence, to redress their grievances.

The principle for which I contend here was fully recognized, I think, by this Court in the opinion delivered by Chief Justice Marshall, in the case of the Blackbird Creek Marsh Co. (Wilson vs. Blackbird Creek Marsh Co., 2 Peters R. 245; and 8 Curtis R. 105.) In that case, a dam had been thrown across a navigable creek by the authority of the State of Delaware, which of course cut off the rights of navigation, and any other rights and privileges, of all who had been accustomed to use the creek. " But this abridgement," said the Chief Justice, " unless it comes in conflict with the Constitution, or a law of the United States, is an affair between the government of Delaware and its citizens, of which this Court can take no cognizance." In other words, a party claiming a right to navigate this Creek under the Constitution, or a law of Congress, may be heard in this Court to complain of the injury. And if the party establish this right of navigation so as to entitle himself to the protection of this Court, he may have his redress, but his redress must be confined to this injury. He cannot go beyond this ground of claim, and ask this Court to entertain his complaints of other alleged greivances, or injuries to other property or business affairs, of his own or of other persons, not under the special protection of the general government, which may be unfavorably affected by the act of the State.

III.

If this case, instead of being looked at, as it must finally be, as necessarily involving the question of public nuisance, should be regarded as involving no judicial question, but that of the private and personal right of the complainants to the free navigation of the Hudson River, the Court I think, would see how impossible it is that this suit in Equity can be maintained. In this view, the case must turn strictly on the question of repugnance to the Constitution, or of a conflict of laws, as between the parties to the record, one party claiming rights under the Constitution of the United States, or a law of Congress, and the other claiming conflicting rights under a State law. Viewing the case in this light, and so it seems to have been viewed by the learned Judge, who first heard the cause—the suit must, I think, be regarded as prematurely brought. Viewed in this light, this is a Bill in Equity, not resting on a charge of public nuisance, which threatens to work a private and irreparable injury to the complainants' property, or interests, but resting on a claim of personal right in which the complainants seek to be quieted by an injunction. I suppose it cannot be doubted that this is a branch of Chancery jurisdiction never exercised except where the right at law is first clearly established. The right is never tried on a Bill in Equity; the right must be settled and undisputed, before a Bill to quiet the right can be entertained.

But in the view of the case now taken, the suit is prematurely brought, not only because the right at law is not settled and undisputed, and therefore cannot be quieted by injunction, but also because, if the Court was disposed to try the right on this Bill in Equity, the question of a conflict of laws, on which the right claimed by the complainants must turn whenever the right is tried, has not arisen, or is not presented in a way to enable the Court to take notice of it.

The Act of the Legislature authorising the bridge, remains without execution, and therefore no actual conflict has arisen or manifested itself, or could do so, between this Legislative Act, and the Act of Congress relied on by the complainants as their warrant of title to the free navigation of the Hudson River.

There can be no question here of repugnance in the Legislative Act, arising on its face, and in its terms, and manifest intent, to any special provision in the Constitution of the United States. We know there are cases in which such repugnance would appear on the face of a State law; as if a State should, without the consent of Congress, lay duties on imports, or a duty of tonnage, in manifest violation of express prohibitions in the Constitution. So a State might pass an Act, which should be, on the face of it, so manifestly designed to be a regulation of commerce in some particular, wherein Congress had already fully legislated, under its power "to regulate commerce" (understood now on all hands to be an exclusive power) that such Legislative Act would be repugnant to the Constitution, because in conflict with the Act of Congress, by its very terms. Such precisely was the conflict of Congressional and State Legislation in the great case of *Gibbons vs Ogden*, [9 Wheaton, R., 240.] The Act of Congress gave authority to all vessels of a certain character, and having a license under that Act, to pass freely, over all the open, navigable waters of the United States, including those of the Bay of New York, and the Hudson River. The Act of the State purported to give authority to a certain class of these same vessels, to navigate the open waters of New York, on having a license under that Act, and forbade all vessels of that particular class to enter upon, or use those waters, without such State authority, under heavy penalties. Nothing could be more palpable than the conflict of laws in this instance, on the face of the Acts themselves.

In all such instances as those now referred to, in a proper judicial case, the Court would have no difficulty in discovering and pronouncing on the repugnancy of the State law to the Constitution, or its conflict with a law of Congress, from the character of the State law. No judicial case *at law*, however, could arise even here, without some act done under the State law to make the occasion or the foundation of a suit. And if a Bill to quiet a right as against such a legislative Act could be maintained at all, it would be on the ground that the right was clear and undisputed by reason of the character of the legislative enactment.

There is, however, a manifest distinction between such cases as I have just referred to, and one where the State legislation complained of has been enacted under an original, undoubted, sovereign power remaining in the State, subject though the power may be, to be restricted and limited by Congressional legislation under another and a different power, and where the Act of State legislation is not, on the face of it, in its terms, or in its plain intent and meaning, or by necessity if carried into execution, repugnant to any provision of the Constitution, or in conflict with any law of Congress.

In such a case it is clear that no action *at law* could be brought by any party in a Court of the United States, so long as no act or proceeding in execution of the State law, or under color of its authority, has taken place to interfere with, or in any manner disturb, the perfect enjoyment of all rights claimed and exercised under the authority of any Act of Congress No foundation could be laid for an action at law. No party could, in an action at law, arraign a naked Act of State legislation before this Court, and ask for its condemnation. He must come here complaining of some wrong, or some loss or damage, for which he holds his adversary responsible.

Take the case before the Court. It is clear that these complainants cannot maintain an action at law in this Court against the Albany Bridge Company. They claim the right of freely navigating the Hudson River at and above Albany, under the authority of an act of Congress, and a license to that effect. But so long as nobody disturbs them in that right, they have no injury or damage to complain of.

No judicial case, then, could be made to give the courts of the United States jurisdiction *at law*, where the question is one of repugnance or conflict, so long as no act or proceeding has taken place under the State legislation resulting in an actual collision of rights and interests. And therefore it is evident that if the Court can entertain a case on a Bill in Equity, where the question is one of repugnance or conflict, before any collision of rights or interests has taken place, then its jurisdiction in Equity stands wholly separated, and apart, from its jurisdiction at law, to this extent; its jurisdiction in Equity precedes its jurisdiction at law in the same identical case, and is exercised when no jurisdiction at law in the same case can be exercised.

The doubt here raised is not to be determined by what may take place in the State Courts under apparently analagous circumstances. The State Courts have general jurisdiction; the Courts of the United States have such special jurisdiction as is given them by the Constitution, and the legislation of Congress. The equity powers of a State Court are a part of its general jurisdiction; the equity powers of the Courts of the United States are a part of its special jurisdiction. In a State, where a party cannot bring a suit at law because he has not yet suffered an actual wrong or injury, but is only threatened with mischief, and therefore brings his suit in Equity, it is entertained, if at all, merely on some rule of Chancery practice. The general jurisdiction of the Court covers the whole case, and if the party cannot be heard on the law side, he may on the Equity side of the Court. But a Court of the United States stands in a very different relation to the same subject. It has a special jurisdiction in cases in law and equity, arising under the Constitution and laws of Congress. A case must arise, before jurisdiction attaches; and, on a question of repugnance or conflict, no case can arise until an actual collision of rights or interests has taken place; and until a case thus arises, the Court has no jurisdiction in law or equity. It is not two jurisdictions over the same question which is given to the Court, but one jurisdiction, to be exercised when a case arises, and the jurisdiction attaches, on the law side, or the equity side, of the Court according to circumstances.

The position which I maintain is, that no question of repugnance or conflict, not apparent on the face of a State law, can properly come before a Court of the United States in a suit originally brought there, until the repugnance or conflict has shown itself in an actual collision of rights or interests. It is doubtful, perhaps, whether the mere passing of an act by a State legislature which the Constitution expressly forbids it to pass, or the mere passing of an act on a subject—the regulation of commerce for example—on which Congress has already legislated, under a power conceded to be exclusive, is sufficient to authorize a Court of the United States to interpose to arrest that Act by a judicial negative, or veto. At least it would seem to be clear that the mere passing of a legislative Act cannot justify such an interposition, when such Act has been passed by a State, under an independent and conceded power, which makes provision for a measure of State policy entirely within its acknowledged competency to provide for ; which is not on the face of it, or by its terms or intent, repugnant to, or in conflict with, the Constitution or any law of Congress ; which must of necessity be a valid Act of legislation both in its inception and maturity, and in its operation, so long as it does not in fact, and by actual collision, conflict, or in any manner interfere with, the fair enjoyment of any rights, property or interests secured by a paramount act of Congress. The case here supposed is precisely the one now before the court. Let us see exactly what this case is, and how it illustrates the question of jurisdiction here presented.

The Act of the Legislature of New York which this Court is called upon to arrest, and forbid being carried into effect, is an Act for establishing, or authorizing, a bridge over the Hudson at Albany. I do not understand that the power of the State to establish a bridge at this point, possessing as it does both banks of the river, and the whole river in its whole extent, is denied or questioned in any quarter. The utmost that is said in derogation of the power is, that it is subject to the power of Congress " to regulate commerce." What that amounts to we shall see.

In the language of Mr. Chief Justice Marshall in *Gibbons vs. Ogden,* this Legislative act " formed a portion of that immense mass of legislation which embraces every thing within the territory of a State not surrendered to the general government ; all which can be most advantageously exercised by the States themselves. Inspection laws, quarantine laws of every description, as well as laws for regulating the internal commerce of a State, and those which respect *turnpike roads, ferries, &c.,* are component parts of this mass."

The power to establish this bridge stands on precisely the same ground as the power to make roads, canals and railways on the land. It is impossible to distinguish between the two cases. If the bridge is subject to the power of Congress over commerce, because it spans a navigable water, so are the highways of commerce on the land, subject to the same power, wherever such highways are, or may be made, routes and channels of foreign or inter-State commerce—a position which I shall have occasion to dwell upon more emphatically for another purpose, in a subsequent part of this argument.

Indeed, the power in these cases is one power, and not two powers. The power to make a road in or through a State, includes the power to make that road continuous by a ferry or a bridge, over a navigable stream. A ferry-boat is a moveable bridge; a bridge is a roadway over a river. Every ferry over a navigable water is an impediment or hindrance to some extent, sometimes to a very great extent, to the use of the highway of the river in the direction of the stream. In some cases, this impediment is vastly greater than a bridge produces, provided with a suitable draw. A bridge is a substitute for a ferry, and whenever a bridge can be conveniently established, with suitable provision for the fair accommodation and use of whatever passes up and down on the highway of the river, such bridge is demanded as a better and more perfect roadway than the ferry. There is hardly one mark of the advancing civilization of the age in which we live, greater or more striking than the vast increase of bridges, and the progressive skill and genius employed in their construction, all over the world. It has been a subject of rival claims to superior civilization and advancement between England and France—the number, magnificence and superiority of the bridges in these countries respectively. What would Paris be without the bridges over the Seine? What would London be without the bridges over the Thames? And these are navigable streams. The Thames is navigable for barges thirty-seven miles above London. Twenty-five years ago, more than three thousand lighters, barges and punts were in use above the lowest London bridge. More steamers bow the heads of their chimneys to the various bridges over the Thames at London, in passing under them, probably in one hour, than would have occasion to pass our bridge at Albany in a week. In the early part of this century, in England, a Parliamentary commission was raised, consisting of twelve members, including the then Speaker, and the Chancellor of the Exchequer, with Thomas Telford, the great architect of the period, as the engineer of the commission, to promote bridge building, especially in the northern district of Scotland, where this civilizing process was more especially needed. In 1812, under the auspices of this commission, 1486 bridges had been constructed, many of them large erections, and some of great magnitude. There is hardly one of the great rivers in the more advanced countries of Western Europe that is without its bridge or bridges, though these rivers almost invariably traverse, or separate, two or more States. A bridge is built, by any sovereign, over any river, on that part of it within his own territory and jurisdiction, he taking care to provide due and fair accommodation for the passing of the bridge by all commerce and navigation in which his own people, or other States, are interested. The government of Prussia has just completed a new and magnificent stone bridge over the Rhine, at Cologne, in place of the bridge of boats which for so many years has occupied that position. This can only be passed by a draw.

In the provision, by a ferry or a bridge, for the crossing of a navigable river, two highways meet and cross each other, just as two highways on the land, running at right angles to each other, meet and cross one another. Two objects meeting at the crossing, cannot occupy the same space on the same, or nearly the same, plane or level. They must accommodate each other, and, if necessary, the police power of the State must step in to regulate the matter.

In all this there is no distinction to be made between the water and the land.

It would be to insist on comparative barbarism, on returning to a state of comparative primitiveness in science, arts and general civilization, to insist, at this day, on the antique and obsolete notion of the superior and monopolizing rights of navigation on navigable streams, as against all rights, or any but the most restricted and meagre rights, of traverse across such streams. The modern railroad, the greatest of all advances made in modern times in physical improvement, giving to commerce and locomotion on the land a facility, rapidity and precision which even steam cannot rival on the water—this must forever put an end to the idea, once perhaps prevalent, that navigation on rivers is entitled to anything more than equal rights, equal privileges, equal facilities, equal protection, with the commerce and travel which follow their great and crowded routes across these rivers.

I venture to state, without fear of contradiction, that, in the very instance before the Court, taking the evidence in the case in spite of all its contradictions and exaggerations, that more tons of freight alone—a great many more—now cross the river at Albany, yearly, in connection with the railroads (and with a bridge the amount will be greatly increased,) than will have occasion to use the draw for passing the bridge up and down the river. Canal boats and barges will pass under the bridge, and so will the whole class of small steam-tugs, with or without a joint in their smoke pipes, without inconvenience. This will leave but comparatively a small part of the navigation employed at or above Albany, to pass the bridge by means of the draw. What in the world is there in sense or reason, what is there that would not be shocking and shameful to sense and reason, to hinder the State and public authorities from according to the vast amount of commerce that traverses the river, even if not half as large as it is, equal protection and equal facilities with that which moves on the river in the direction of the stream? And if some of the commerce in these two branches must submit to partial inconveniences, what is there in sense or reason, to justify the laying of the whole burthen on that which traverses the river, and none at all on that which employs navigation in the direction of the stream?

And, then, for the persons who are to be accommodated in traversing, and those in passing up and down the river at this point. The comparison is, of three to four thousand daily of those who cross the river at this point, to less than 150 who pass up and down. Can anybody suggest a reason why the government should not take care of the rights and interests of the three or four thousand, as well as of the 150—of the million and more of passengers yearly in one direction, as well as of the 35,000 in the other direction?—especially while in one case the travel, with all the vast business and social interests connected with it, flows on steadily from years' end to years' end, and in the other it is periodical, and is wholly suspended for three or more months in the year.

If the power to make roads, canals and railways is a conceded and indispensable power belonging to the State, which it would be a shameful dereliction of governmental duty not to exercise, to the extent of its ability, it must be equally a conceded and indispensable power belonging to it, to establish bridges over the navigable waters within its territorial sovereignty and jurisdiction, wherever they are practicable, and the public interest demands them, and which it would equally be a shameful dereliction of duty not to exercise. I know of no distinction that can be made between the waters within the territorial limits of the State, and the land, in regard to soveregnty and jurisdiction in the State Government. There can be no greater error, in my judgment, than to suppose that the Constitution of the United States, by any of its provisions, or by any inference to be drawn from the character, necessities or objects of the government established by it, takes from the State its general sovereignty and jurisdiction over its navigable waters, any more, or in any greater degree, than it takes from it its general sovereignty and jurisdiction on the land. The State is sovereign over the waters in the same sense, and in the same degree, that it is on the land. As sovereign, it commands in all public places, as on highways and rivers. A river is a highway devoted to the use of the public, just in the same sense in which a road is a highway devoted to the use of the public. That grand and comprehensive provision of the Constitution, that " the citizens of each State shall be entitled to all privileges and immunities of citizens of the several States," which so beautifully constitutes the people of the United States one people, without trenching on the separate communities into which they are divided, or the general sovereignty of the governments of those communities, undoubtedly enlarges that public to whose use the navigable waters of the several States are devoted, from the public of the State to the public of the United States. And in exactly the same manner, and in the same degree, are the highways of a State devoted to the use of the whole people of the United States, instead of being limited to the people of the State. No State can impose any restrictions, terms or conditions, on citizens of other States, in the use of its highways, whether of water or on land, than such as it imposes on its own citizens. And it can give its own citizens no privileges, immunities or advantages in the use of these highways, that do not at once, and equally, belong to the citizens of all the States. But the State, as sovereign, does not the less command in these public places, as it does elsewhere, within its territorial limits.

The boundaries of the State of New York include all the waters of the great Bay of New York as far as Sandy Hook, or to the open sea, and the waters of the Sound to the eastern line of the State across that arm of the sea ; and of course they include all its interior waters. Within all these boundaries, water and land included, the State is everywhere Sovereign. It is sovereign in the same sense in which it was sovereign before the Constitution, notwithstanding the surrender of certain specified powers which it cannot now exercise at all, and notwithstanding the fact that among its general powers not surrendered, there are some of which the exercise is subject to restriction and limitation by the exercise of some power on the part of the general government which has been surrendered. The State has not lost its general sovereignty and jurisdiction because it has surrendered its independent power to lay duties on imports and exports, and to lay duties of tonnage; nor because its power to legislate in respect to its public highways, whether of water or on land, may be subject, in a certain degree, to the paramount power of Congress "to regulate commerce;" nor because the judiciary of the United States is clothed exclusively with the admiralty and maritime jurisdiction of the country. In this latter particular, this Court has said that this power does not carry a cession of the water where these cases may arise, or the general jurisdiction over them. This adheres to the territory, and to the government to which the territory belongs. (U. S. vs. Bevans, 3 Wheat. R. 316.)

The State owns the soil under all the navigable waters within its boundaries—taking the term "navigable" in its common law meaning, as applied to waters where the tide flows and ebbs. The State owns the soil under the navigable waters of the Bay of New York, and of the Hudson, and it grants the soil at its pleasure. (Commissioners of Canal Fund vs. Kempshall; 26 Wendell's R. p. 414; Verplank's opinion.) The Commissioners of the Land Office have power to grant these lands, and have frequently exercised that power. The State has granted the land under water around the city of New York, to that city, for the purpose of constructing piers, wharves and docks for the uses of commerce, at that great centre of trade and navigation. At other points and places on the Hudson, the State has made similar grants for similar uses. The State itself constructed the great pier and basin at Albany, in connection with its canals, and has granted land under the water on the opposite side of the river at this place, for piers and wharves. And wherever such grants have been made, encroachments have necessarily been made to some extent, on the bed and highway, and public easement, of these navigable waters. And nobody that I have heard of, has thought of questioning the sovereignty and jurisdiction of the State in this matter, or its right to grant the land, and to authorize these encroachments on the free flow and navigation of the river. The general goverment itself has received frequent cessions from the State, by formal transactions, both of the soil under these same waters, and of the general jurisdiction (with some special reserves) over the sites thus ceded. It has received these cessions in the Bay of New York, and at various points in the Hudson River, for light houses, and other erections, necessary for national uses.

Some years ago the State authorised a bridge over the Hudson at Troy. This was opposed by those interested in the navigation above Troy, where the tide flows, but after a trial in the State Court, and a decision, accompanied by a very learned and able opinion, in favor of the right, the opposition was abandoned, and there the bridge now stands, with only a very narrow and inconvenient draw, for the accommodation of the navigation above it. Many years ago the State, in connection with its canals, constructed a dam across the river at a point below the flow of the tide, with a lock through which all navigation above has to pass.

In virtue of the same sovereignty and jurisdiction, which the State has been exercising ever since the Union was formed, it has now undertaken to establish a bridge at

Albany. This is opposed, almost of course, by those who are interested in the navigation above this point, and by the parties most interested in maintaining the bridge at Troy.

I do not understand, however, that the general sovereignty and jurisdiction of the State, over the waters of the river are denied, or the general right to make or authorise erections therein, provided the freedom of navigation be preserved. What is insisted on, is, that the right to establish a bridge is subject to the power of Congress to regulate commerce; that Congress has legislated under this power in the Act for granting licenses for the coasting trade; that the complainants, and others, are engaged in navigating the river under the authority of such licenses; that these licenses secure to them the right to the free and unobstructed navigation of the river, at and above Albany; and that in their opinion, and in the opinion of *their* witnesses, the bridge, if built, will not leave to them, what they consider a free and unobstructed navigation.

The bridge, it must be remembered, has not been erected; it was not erected, or begun, when this suit was brought, and it has not yet been erected, or begun, because two years and a half ago, the judicial power of the United States, was successfully invoked to lay the State, or its agents, under interdict against the erection. The State, by the very terms and conditions of its enactment, had made the most careful and anxious provisions for preserving and maintaining " the free navigation " of the river—a matter in which the State had quite as deep a stake as any body else, in or out of the State, could have. The free navigation was to be preserved, first by the elevation of the bridge " so as to allow under it the free passage of canal boats, and barges without masts," in which, in truth, the great bulk of the commerce above Albany is borne; and next, by a draw, or draws, " of sufficient width to admit the free passage of the largest vessels navigating the river."

The Act, with its supplement, fixes the minimum width of the draw, or draws, which must therefore be of the most ample width, and such as could only be constructed by the advance and triumphs of modern science and skill. Other provisions are made for rendering voluntary aid, without cost, by means of steam tugs, to facilitate vessels in passing the draws of the bridge; and other provisions still, for the prompt application of remedial measures for keeping the bed and channel of the river free, if by possible chance, the piers of the bridge should be found to cause any obstruction in them. Finally, the Act provides, under severe penalties for any neglect, for the prompt and efficient management of the bridge, and of the draw or draws, to accommodate and facilitate vessels in a safe and easy passage through the bridge, at all times of the day and night.

Now it is in the face of all these careful provisions, embodied in the Act itself, for preserving the free navigation of the river, before the erection of the bridge is begun, and before the right or interest of any human being, as claimed under an act of Congress, has been in any manner encroached upon or disturbed, that a question of repugnance to the Constitution, or of conflict with such act of Congress, in the law of the State authorizing the bridge, has been raised, which the Courts of the United States have been asked to entertain, and, upon the anticipation of events that no mortal man can say will ever happen, and, on testimony, of necessity and in the nature of the subject, amounting to nothing but a purely speculative prognostication of evil, to forbid the law of the State being carried into effect.

Now, what I insist upon is, that no question of repugnance or conflict has arisen in this case of which the Court can take cognizance; that no judicial case can arise, where the question is one of repugnance or conflict, not apparent on the face of the legislative Act, until an actual collision of rights or interests takes place in the working or operation of the law against which repugnance or conflict is alleged; that no judicial case can arise, in law or equity, on an allegation of repugnance or conflict, upon a naked or unexecuted law of a State; that if it can arise where the repugnance or conflict is palpable on the face of the law, it cannot arise, on such an allegation, upon a naked or unexecuted law of a State, where that law, on its face, and in its terms, and plain intent and meaning, is confessedly not repugnant to the Constitution, or in conflict with any act of Congress; and that the Court cannot create a judicial case for itself, nor can parties create a judicial case for it, when the case is such as I have described, by means of allegations, and volumes of proofs, offered and received, to show that it is intended to carry the law into effect, and that, if carried into effect, apprehensions and opinions are entertained that certain rights or interests claimed under au Act of Congress, will or may be impaired or disturbed, and thus a conflict between the law of the State and such Act of Congress would or might be established. I hold that the Court cannot anticipate a conflict of laws in any case; that there is no conflict of laws in a case like this before the Court, of which the Court can take cognizance, until an actual collision of rights and interests takes place to show the conflict, and to lay the ground for a judicial case; that the Court must wait until the rights or interests of some party, claiming under the authority of the United States, have been impaired or disturbed by some party acting under the State law, or is alleged to have been so, before it can entertain so grave a question as that of conflict between the two laws, and the two governments enacting them respectively, and where the result may be the condemnation of the law of the State, upon mere speculation as to its operation, and the arrest of the government of the State, in a measure which may be of vital importance to the interests and prosperity of the people over which its sovereignty is exercised.

If a naked, and as yet unexecuted, State law can be brought under the revision of the National Judiciary, in the form of a proceeding in Equity, and there forbidden to be carried into effect, not from what may appear on the face of the law, but from testimony received to show what will be its probable, or possible, operation if not thus forbidden, then I think no one can fail to see that the Judiciary, in all such cases, performs an office quite foreign to its character as a Judiciary—an anomalous office, partly executive and partly legislative, and such as we must all be quite sure was never intended to be created, or bestowed, on any branch of the National Government.

The subject of vesting just such an authority in Congress, or in some other hands to be devised for the purpose, was proposed, and very earnestly debated, in the Convention which framed the Constitution of the United States. There was hardly any other single topic which was longer under debate, or more deliberately considered. Congress was the body in whose hands it was generally thought best to lodge the power of revision and veto, over State legislation; though suggestions were made of a Commissioner for this purpose to reside in each State, or to make the Governors of the States appointees of the General Government, and clothe them with the power of revision and an absolute veto. Many of the leading men in the Convention advocated such a power, Mr. Madison, perhaps, more persistently than anybody else. The main object was the exercise of the very identical power we are now considering—that of revising and arresting, by an absolute negative, all State laws which might be deemed to be repugnant to the Constitution, or in conflict, or likely to come into conflict, with any law of Congress. Of course, the question of repugnance or conflict was to arise on the naked law, before it should be carried into effect, and was to be determined upon the character and provisions of the law itself, or upon such an inquest, and such investigations into the probable, or possible, operation of the law, if allowed to be carried into effect, as should satisfy the revising authority. It was not until a late period in the session of the Constitutional Convention that this project was abandoned. It was not abandoned until its advocates became satisfied that the States would indignantly reject any Constitution containing such a provision—one which would have effectually stripped them of all proper sovereignty, and left them with no more authority or dignity than a Board of Supervisors in a county. Fortunately, when the powers to be given to the Judiciary of the United States, came at last to be adjusted and settled, and the language carefully selected and fixed by which those powers were created and conferred ; when it was seen that its authority extended to all judicial cases arising under the Constitution, laws and treaties of the United States, and when, finally, the important and vital principle and provision was added that the Constitution, laws and treaties of the United States should be the supreme law of the land, " anything in the Constitution or laws of any State to the contrary notwithstanding ;" when all this was done, all parties became satisfied that a much better, wiser and safer adjustment had been made of the difficult and delicate problem of securing harmony between the State Governments and their laws, and the Constitution and laws of the United States, than could have been done by any direct power of revision and negative over State legislation. (Vide Curtis Hist. of Constitution, vol 2, pp. 430, 437, 438, 439 and 440; 5 Elliot's Debates, pp. 170–4, 209, 210, 251, 321, 468, 469, 539, and Index, tit. "Acts," p. 604)

It will not do to say that this power of revision and negative was merely shifted from Congress, where it was first proposed to lodge it, to the Judiciary. No such power was conferred by the Constitution, and if it had been, and had been so understood, that instrument would certainly have been rejected by the States. The power in the hands of the Judiciary would certainly not have been deemed less exceptionable than in the hands of Congress. Where inquisition and investigations are to be made, and volumes of testimony taken and weighed, on subjects so peculiarly of parliamentary or legislative cognizance, as in the very case now under review in this Court, before a question of repugnance or conflict alleged against a State law can be decided; certainly no one can say that such a case is not fitter for a parliamentary committee than for the Judiciary. Must not every one say that it is fit only for such a committee, and for legislative action and determination, and not at all for a judicial body? Certainly, every one must see that the true way and the only way—a method perfectly effectual too for all practical purposes—of dealing with this subject of State legislation, to keep it in practical harmony with the Constitution and laws of the United States, and at the same time relieve the necessary interference with it, in cases of alleged repugnance or conflict, of all that is most offensive to the dignity and sovereignty of the State, was the very course adopted by the Constitution. By this means, all State legislation, passed under admitted powers, stands as valid law, on the authority of the sovereignty which enacts it, until a conflict declares itself by some actual collision of rights and interests between parties, claiming respectively under State legislation and under the Constitution or legislation of Congress, and then the Judiciary is invoked to settle the question on a judicial case, and in a strictly judicial way. (2 Curtis Hist. of Const., p. 54.)

It adds, I think, force to the view I have ventured to present on this subject, that previous to the Albany Bridge Case, no occasion had ever been found on which it was thought proper to employ a Preliminary Injunction to arrest a State law, as yet but a naked and unexecuted enactment, and a valid law on the face of it, on an allegation of repugnance or conflict. And if the Injunction should be made perpetual, it would be the first example and instance of such a conclusion being reached, in any similar case. If I am mistaken in this, the Court will know. I have not found or heard of such a case.

In the leading case of Gibbons vs. Ogden the collision of rights and interests was actual and flagrant when the injuction was asked for and granted in the State Court, and of course when the case came before this Court on appeal.

In the Blackbird Creek case, (8 Curtis, 105,) a dam had been constructed across the creek, and a collision in respect to rights and interests had occurred.

Applications for Injunctions to prevent the erection of bridges over navigable waters have been asked for in several instances, and the Courts have entertained the cases—the question of jurisdiction not having been raised. It seems to have been assumed that the Court had the power to grant the Injunction, if a case for it was made out; but no such Injunction has been granted, I think, in any case. Yet the distinction does not seem to have been adverted to, between the act of a mere trespasser in placing obstructions in a public river, complained of in an English Court of Chancery as threatening injury to an unquestioned private right, and erections authorized by State legislation, which, on its face, contemplates no unlawful obstruction, and which, as I hold, cannot be complained of in this Court, by a private party claiming under a law of Congress, so long as his right, whatever it be, remains actually undisturbed.

In the Cuyahoga River Bridge case, before Mr. Justice McLean, (3 McLean R. 226) the complainant relied on the ordinance of 1787, for his claim to the free navigation of this river, which he insisted would be obstructed by a draw bridge. The application was denied.

In the Rock Island Bridge case, before the same judge, (4 McLean's R. 517) the application for an injunction was denied. There the United States was a party, and complained not only of prospective injury to the navigation, if the bridge should be erected—a ground of claim in the case which the Court declared the United States as a private party could not set up—but complained also of special injury, already done by excavations and otherwise, to Rock Island, of which the United States was proprietor. The case turned on this latter complaint.

In the cases arising in New Jersey before Mr. Justice Grier, (vol., Alb. Bridge case, 74) the application for injunctions was denied. In these cases there was a complaint of the proposed erections as public nuisances, and they appear to have been considered in that view.

In the Wheeling Bridge case, (19 Curtis R. 621) the application for an injunction to prevent the bridge being built, was in behalf of Pennsylvania, and was put expressly on the ground of nuisance. Before the case came to a hearing the bridge had been completed, and a supplemental Bill set forth that fact, and complained of the bridge, not as a prospective, but as an actual nuisance, doing special damage to the complainant. On this ground the case appears to have been heard and decided.

In the case now before the Court, on the hearing for a Preliminary Injunction, Mr. Justice Nelson appears to have considered the case as analagous to cases in the English Court of Chancery, where the title of the complainant was clear, but the obstructions denied, and where the question of obstruction or not, was the only one to be tried. These were cases of unauthorized obstructions by individual enterprise. And even there, Chancery would not try the question of obstruction, which here the Circuit Court proposed to do, and thereupon issued the Injunction till the further hearing on that point in Equity.

The Court regarded the Complainants as having an unquestioned "legal right to a free and unobstructed navigation of the Hudson River, secured by the Constitution and Acts of Congress;" and stated that the right was understood not to be denied on the argument.

The mistake in this statement, I suppose, consists in inadvertently stating the "legal right" supposed to be conceded, altogether too broadly. The right to navigate the river was admitted, but the right to build the bridge, just as authorized by legislative enactment, was insisted on at the same time, and any right of navigation which could not be enjoyed with such a bridge, was not admitted, but denied. The legal right of the complainant " to a free and unobstructed navigation," in the broad sense of these terms, was not therefore clear, and was not unquestioned. There was an admitted right of navigation, but not in exclusion of the bridge, and just such a bridge as the State law contemplated. The bridge as contemplated, would leave all the navigation the complainant was entitled to, and any larger right of navigation than this was denied. This was the defendant's position.

Here were opposing claims of right under the legislation of different governments. The laws in both cases were passed by perfectly competent authority; and no supremacy could be asserted for the law, under which the complainants claimed, over the law under which the defendant claimed, until the right of the complainants, whatever it might be, was encroached upon by the measure adopted under the State law. The laws themselves did not conflict; and no case, as I suppose, could be made for the Court until an actual collision of rights, or what might be claimed to be such, should take place. Then an action at law would decide between the opposing claims.

But all this was anticipated by the Court. On a Bill in Equity, a broad, and disputed right of navigation, but still undefined, was held to belong to the complainants. And, thereupon, though the State law contemplated no obstruction to any reasonable right of navigation, testimony was received on the one side and the other, on which the Court might try the question, whether, or not, an unlawful obstruction to the vague right of navigation as held by the

Court to belong to the complainants, might not be created if the bridge should be constructed.

We hold that the Court, on this Bill in Equity, if considered merely as a Bill to quiet a right by injunction, erred in entertaining either the question of right, or the question of obstruction.

IV.

But I suppose it is not to be doubted that all these cases where suits are brought in Equity to protect the rights and interests of the complainants in the navigation of public rivers against bridges, and the like erections, if they can be maintained at all, must stand on the charge of public nuisance against the alleged obstructions, and cannot rest on any other ground of Chancery jurisdiction. It is not an isolated private right which is set up in these cases. It is a right enjoyed in common with the public, or at least such portion of the public as have a common authority from the Government of the United States. What is complained of, along with the injury to a personal right, is an unlawful obstruction of a public navigable river, or common highway. This is a public nuisance, according to the doctrine of the common law.

The complainants in the case before the Court, have not neglected in their Bills to declare that the bridge, if erected, will be a common nuisance. In my further consideration of this case, I shall treat it as standing on this ground.

The first question to be considered, is, whether the Court has jurisdiction and authority to declare an obstruction to navigation, actual or threatened, in a public river, placed there without the authority of the United States, to be a public nuisance.

I have referred already to several cases in which the Court seemed to take this jurisdiction for granted. The question of jurisdiction does not appear to have been raised.

In the Wheeling Bridge case, it is not to be denied that a majority of the Court held the bridge, as erected, to be a public nuisance, because in their judgment it obstructed the accustomed use of the River Ohio, to a certain class of vessels, navigating that river ; and the right of the Court to entertain the case on a Bill in Equity, as a question of nuisance was elaborately maintained. Two members of the Court, however, dissented from this opinion, the Chief Justice being one of them, who utterly denied the jurisdiction.

As this was the first case, and is thus far I believe the only one, in which this question of jurisdiction was considered, I hope it may not be thought going too far, to ask that the question should not be deemed settled past all propriety of reconsidering it. Perhaps that case might be advantageously reconsidered, in more aspects than one. The decision was by a divided Court. The decree in the case, was never carried into effect, because Congress interposed by a special Act of Legislation, under its power to establish post-roads, to affirm the State Legislation in the premises, as not illegal, and not creating a nuisance, and to adopt the bridge, just as it was built, as a post-road. And I suppose all parties and persons, are now satisfied that it would have been a great misfortune, and a great calamity, not to Virginia only, but to the whole country, if the erection of that bridge had been prevented, or if being erected, it had been abated by the Court, as a nuisance. The case, therefore, as a whole, is hardly one to be followed as a precedent.

The majority of the Court put the right of the complainant, the State of Pennsylvania, to complain of the bridge, on the ground of private injury from a public nuisance. She did not sue in her capacity of a sovereign State. She was before the Court in the position and light of any natural person, or ordinary corporation. She was not engaged in navigating the river under a license from the United States, and therefore could not complain that her rights of navigation under a law of Congress, were interfered with. But the right of all the people of the United States to the free navigation of the river was insisted on, as having been somehow or other secured by the legislation of Congress. Regulations of commerce by Congress, under which licenses for the coasting trade had been granted, and ports of entry established on the river, were referred to; and so was the compact between Virginia and Kentucky in relation to the free navigation of the Ohio, and the sanction of that compact by Congress. This compact seems to have been mainly relied on as establishing the general right of free navigation under the authority of Congress. But the complainant, as a legal person or corporation, who was not engaged in the navigation of the river in any way, and who had therefore no violated rights in that particular to complain of, could not make a judicial case for itself in this Court on that ground. If the legislation of Congress secured the free navigation of the river to all who chose to navigate it, and if the legislation of Virginia authorizing the bridge, was in conflict with that right, still the complainant was not engaged in the navigation, and no individual rights of hers in that respect had been disturbed by the bridge. And since she could not claim the protection of the Court against the legislation of Virginia as being herself engaged in navigating the river, under the authority of Congress, she was in no condition to invoke that protection for others who were thus engaged. It was not, then, her individual right of navigation which was complained of as interfered with by an obstruction constituting a public nuisance. She set up certain losses and damage to her interests in works of internal improvement of which she was proprietor, as flowing directly from the obstruction, and on this ground of private injury from the obstruction, which she charged as a nuisance, her case rested.

The jurisdiction of the Court in this view of the case was, as I have said, elaborately maintained. It seems to have been put mainly on the ground that this Court had adopted the practice of the high Court of Chancery in England, where jurisdiction in analagous cases was entertained. But the question of jurisdiction in this Court was entirely distinct from any mere question of chancery practice. The question whether, on a Bill in Equity, this Court will proceed according to the practice of State Courts, or according to the practice of the Court of Chancery in England, does not seem to me to meet the question of jurisdiction. The Court say, "the usages of the high Court of Chancery, *whenever the jurisdiction is exercised*, govern the proceedings." But this does not go one step towards deciding whether the jurisdiction in this case can be exercised by this Court, according to law. If it cannot, no usages or practice of any Court can be applied to it.

The jurisdiction of the Courts of the United States is special and not general, and is just what the Constitution and laws of Congress confer on them, and this is as true of their jurisdiction in equity as in law. In Wheaton and Donaldson vs. Peters, (8 Peters, 658,) the Court said : "It is clear there can be no common law of the United States. There is no principle which pervades the Union, and has the authority of law, that is not embodied in the Constitution or laws of the Union. The common law could be made a part of our federal system only by legislative adoption. When, therefore, a common law right is asserted, we must look to the State in which the controversy originated."

This Court must have some law to give it jurisdiction. It has no general common law jurisdiction. Its authority to pronounce the bridge a nuisance must rest on the legislation of Congress; either on such legislation directly applied to the subject, or on the Act of Congress which makes the laws of the State where the controversy originated, the rule of decision in a Court of the United States. If there had been any legislation of Congress which made this bridge, as partially obstructing the free navigation of the Ohio, a public nuisance, or if the common law of Virginia as modified by the Statute authorizing the bridge, made the bridge a public nuisance, then the Court had jurisdiction so to pronounce; otherwise it had no jurisdiction.

It cannot be pretended that the bridge was a nuisance by the laws of Virginia. No State Court of Virginia could have so pronounced. No Court of the United States, sitting in that State, could have so pronounced. A Statute of the State had authorized the bridge, and that was the end of the law in that State, so far as the allegation of public nuisance was concerned.

Upon what legislation of Congress, then, applicable directly to the subject, could the complainant rely to maintain the jurisdiction of the Court.

It is not pretended that there was any enactment of Congress, in terms, declaring obstructions, partial or otherwise, in navigable rivers generally, or in the Ohio in particular, whether by bridges, or other erections, public nuisances. There was no direct Legislation of Congress, on the subject of bridges over navigable waters; none defining what erections should constitute, or be deemed, obstructions, and what should not, or what obstructions should be deemed a nuisance, and what should not. And it is difficult to conceive how this Court could have jurisdiction to define and declare what erections in a navigable river, should be deemed obstructions, and public nuisances, and what should not, while it is certain that Congress, from which alone its authority on the subject must be derived, has never Legislated on the subject of obstructions to navigable rivers in any form whatever.

A public nuisance is a public offence, and those who establish or maintain it, are liable to indictment and punishment as public offenders. There can be no public nuisance which is not a public offence. And there can be no better test of the right of jurisdiction in this Court, in a civil case, to declare any act complained of a nuisance, than to enquire if any legislation of Congress, has declared that act to be a public offence. The Court in this case concede that it has no criminal jurisdiction in the matter, because Congress has passed no law, declaring the act of establishing such a bridge a public offence, and prescribing the punishment of it. Certainly, that is an abundantly good reason why the Court cannot exercise criminal jurisdiction in the case; but it is an equally good reason, why a civil suit cannot be maintained for a private injury arising from the act complained of. If there is no legislation of Congress, which makes the erection of a bridge obstructing navigation, a public nuisance and offence, whether provision is made, or not, for its punishment criminally, then certainly no private suit can be maintained for special damage, arising from it, on the ground of its being a public nuisance. It cannot be held to be a public offence, except by the legislation of Congress. There is confesedly no such direct legislation. There is nothing, therefore, to warrant the Court in deeming the bridge to be a public nuisance, or treating it as such.

At common law, the unauthorised obstruction of a navigable river, is a public offence, and punishable by indictment. (4. Bl. com. 167.) But, as we have seen, there can be no common law offence of this kind against the United States. Ten thousand obstructions of navigable rivers in the United States might be made, without one public offence against the United States, until Congress shall declare any such act to be a public offence. Obstructing the mails of the United States, is not a public offence, until Congress so declares it. Counterfeiting the coin of the United States is not a public offence, till Congress so declares it. Surely the Courts of the United States, have no larger authority over the navigable waters of the United States, within the territorial limits of the several States, than they have over the public mails, and the public coin, in the absence or want of legislation by Congress, to provide for their protection. If Congress has thought, as it might well think, that the States themselves were the best authorities to protect their public waters against unauthorsed obstructions, and that serious obstructions of their own navigable rivers by State authority, was too remote a probability or possibillity, to require any legislation on the part of Congress, certainly, there can be neither any authority, or any occasion, for the Courts of the United States to intervene in the matter.

It seems to me to be sufficient to rest the objections to the jurisdiction entertained by the Court in the Wheeling Bridge case, where I have now placed them. But I shall have occasion to recur to that case in another part of my argument, and to present some further views which cannot fail, I think, to add strength to those already submitted.

It is most apparent to my mind, that the Court in the Wheeling Bridge case, in declaring the bridge over the Ohio to be an unlawful obstruction, and a public nuisance, as against the sovereign rights and authority of the United States—for the decision was exactly that, or it was nothing—declared what Congress had never declared, and had never authorized the Court to declare. I hope I shall be believed when I say, that in submitting my views of that case, I do so without any abatement whatever of the profound respect for this Court which it has been the habit and the pride of my whole life to entertain. I confess, at the same time, to the deepest anxiety, as a matter of the highest importance to great public interests, that that case shall not be deemed by this Court as a settled precedent for the leading doctrines which may be thought to be embraced in the decision, and certainly not as establishing the jurisdiction and authority of the Court, without some more explicit legislation of Congress on the subject than any we now have, to declare what shall, and what shall not, be deemed obstructions in a public river, and when any such obstruction shall, and when it shall not, be deemed a public nuisance.

To come back now to the case before the Court. I ask the Court to apply to this case, the reasoning I have ventured to employ in reference to the Wheeling Bridge case.

If I do not greatly deceive myself, it is quite clear, that this Court has no authority to decide that a bridge, erected by State authority, over a navigable river within the territorial limits of the State, is an obstruction to the navigation of such a character as to be a public nuisance. It has no such authority, because Congress has not given it any such authority, and it has no common law jurisdiction in such cases, or in any case. Congress has passed no laws to forbid obstructions in public rivers, or to declare any obstruction a public nuisance. I go further than this, and maintain that it has adopted no legislation the object of which has been to control State legislation over the navigable rivers within the limits of a State, in respect to erections, such as piers, wharves and bridges, in or over such rivers, or in ·respect to any effect which may be produced by such erections upon the freedom of navigation. But I shall have more to say on this last position in another part of this argument.

V.

The Court cannot, of course, interpose to prevent the creation of a public nuisance, at the instance of a private party, unless that party shows that some special damage or injury will accrue to some personal right, property or interest of his own, from the nuisance. For this reason, and to give the complainants the right to prosecute their complaint in this Court instead of a State Court, they allege that they have a special right to the personal use and enjoyment of the free navigation of the river under a license for the coasting trade, issued to them, respectively, under the authority of an Act of Congress, and that the bridge, if erected, will greatly interfere with, and limit, the use and enjoyment of such licenses. They also insist that the bridge will derange, interrupt and diminish, and do irreparable injury to the trade, commerce and business, connected with the navigation of the river, in which they are personally engaged. And one of them complains that the bridge will greatly and irretrievably impair the value of his real and personal property in Troy.

Having thus, as they suppose, established their personal right to complain of the proposed bridge as a public nuisance, they ask for the interposition of the Court to forbid its erection.

But several things are necessary to be established before the Court can interpose in the way demanded. It must appear:

That the proposed bridge will, if established, be a public nuisance;

That the allegations of special damage or injury to the complainants, as set forth by them, or that some of them, are such as this Court can take cognizance of;

That the right or interest, the injury to which is complained of, is a clear right or interest at law, in the complainants; and,

That that right or interest is of such a nature, and the injury of such a character, and extent or degree, that adequate redress could not be had in an action at law.

I have already shown, or endeavored to show, that the Court cannot take cognizance of any allegations of the complainants, to make them a substantive ground of judicial action, which consist of complaints that the erection of the proposed bridge threatens to impair the value of their real and personal property in Troy, and to injure their general business affairs and interests, carried on at that city, or elsewhere. Much less can the Court take such cognizance of any allegations of the complainants to the effect that the State had entered on a measure of mistaken public policy, which, instead of benefitting, would inflict injury on its own public interests, and on its own people, either generally, or in particular localities.

The general charge in the case is that of public nuisance by obstructing a public river—in other words, a charge that the defendant is about to do an act criminal in its nature, an act which would be an offence against the United States.

None of the allegations of private injury to the complainants, in this case, can be received, as putting them in a position to bring this charge of public nuisance against the proposed bridge, in the form of a Bill for an Injunction, except that which affirms their personal right, under the authority of an act of Congress, to the free navigation of the river. It is the right to the use and enjoyment of the license they set up, and of the free navigation of the river under it, which they insist would be directly interfered with by the proposed bridge, which gives them the right, if any they have, to complain of the bridge as a public nuisance.

It must be remembered that the only public nuisance of which this Court could take cognizance, in any form of action, information or complaint, is, a public nuisance, and a public offence, against the government of the United States. A nuisance and offence against a State government is not within its cognizance. The proper mode, undoubtedly, of bringing before this Court a charge of nuisance committed, or threatened, against the United States, would be upon an Information, to which the Attorney General of the United States should be a party. (Opinion of Ch. J. Taney, in the Wheeling Bridge case, 19 Custis, p. 655.) The United States is the principal party in interest in the question of such nuisance, and ought to be heard, by its proper officer, before the question of nuisance, or no nuisance, should be decided. And the only ground on which a Court of Chancery will hear this charge of public nuisance from a private party (if it ought to or will hear it at all) is that of a direct, immediate and irreparable injury, actual or threatened, to the use and enjoyment of some right, property or interest of such party, and for the redress of which an action at law would be inadequate. Allegations of remote, contingent, incidental or speculative interests, will not be listened to. Besides, on a Bill in Equity in a Court of the United States, such private party could only be heard to complain of private injury to the use and enjoyment of some right, property or interest held and enjoyed under the Constitution or Laws of the United States.

In this case, the complainants must stand on the particular right claimed by them to the free navigation of the river, under the authority of their license from the United States, and the allegation that the use and enjoyment of such license and right will be directly interfered with, and injured, by the bridge, and nuisance, if permitted to be established.

On this state of the case, the question presents itself whether the particular private injury here set forth, if any should ever accrue from the erection of the bridge, is not one for which an adequate and complete redress could be had in an action at law. If it could, it is clear upon the unquestioned doctrine of the law on the subject, that the complainants cannot be heard to bring this charge of nuisance against the bridge on this Bill in Equity for an Injunction. There is, besides, a statute of the United States forbidding the Courts to entertain a case in equity when a plain and adequate remedy in the case may be had at law. (1 Stats. at large, 73.)

Of the adequacy of the remedy at law in this case, there cannot be a doubt. Nobody pretends that the bridge is to shut up the river. The complainants will always be able to take their vessels through the draw. If they experience all the difficulty, delay and danger which their worst apprehensions anticipate, there will still be no difficulty in ascertaining their loss and damage in an action at law. The loss by delays, whether of minutes or days, and the loss from injuries to vessels or cargoes, by collisions with the bridge or otherwise, and any extra expense attending the passage, are all as easily ascertainable in dollars and cents, as damages in a thousand other cases constantly tried in our courts. The losses ascertained on one occasion would be a guide to the amount of the like losses on other occasions. And even the amount of damage sustained by depreciation in the value of the complainant's property, real or personal, in Troy, or by lessening the profits of their general business—if these remote and incidental effects of the bridge, supposing them to occur, could be made the subject of claims for damages at all—could be ascertained without any special difficulty.

The complainants cannot be heard in this case as the representatives of a class—those navigating the river under licenses for the coasting trade, for example; or as the representatives of the navigating interest generally on the Hudson; or as the representatives of Troy, West Troy and Green Island. They cannot be heard to ask the Court to forbid the erection of the bridge, in the interest of the public, and because it will be a public nuisance. If the Court arrest the erection, it will not be to protect the public, or any portion of the public, from the bridge as a public nuisance. The government which represents the public, and is the guardian of its interests, is not before the Court, and has not complained of the bridge as a nuisance, or asked the Court for its interposition. Until it does so, the Court cannot volunteer to be the guardians of the public interests in this regard. The Court can only consider the question of public nuisance, or not, in the interest of the complainants, and not at all in the interest of the public, and if it puts its interdict on the bridge, it must be for the protection of the complainants, and for them alone. (Opinion of Ch. J. Taney, in Wheeling bridge case, 19 Custis, p. 655.) The question for the Court, in this view, is, whether the extraordinary protection which the complainants demand is indispensible in order to secure them in the enjoyment of rights and interests which, of themselves alone, are of such great magnitude, and such pressing importance, and at the same time are of such a character, that a remedy at law could not reach or cover them with any adequate redress. To propound such a question is to answer it.

The misfortune of this case, brought before the Court on a Bill for an Injunction, is, that if the Court grants the Injunction to protect the complainants, it forecloses the public, and the government of the United States as representing the public, on the question of the charge against the bridge as a public nuisance, without that public being allowed to be heard on that question, as it is entitled to be heard. The fact that the government of the United States, against which this offence of nuisance is committed, if it be a nuisance, has not complained, and does not complain of it, through its proper officer, should be taken to bear strongly against all present interference with it. The complainants have no right to ask the Court to interpose for their individual protection in a mode which, if their suit is successful, forecloses the public on the main issue in the case, without suit or a hearing on its part, while the law is open to them, by a plain remedy for full redress, whenever they are touched by any actual injury to their personal rights or interests from the establishing of the bridge. If not satisfied with their remedy at law, and if, moreover, they really think the bridge will be a public nuisance, and a public crime, and are really desirous that the public as well as themselves, shall be protected from it, let them apply to the Attorney General of the United States, the proper law officer of the government, to institute and prosecute proceedings in behalf of the the government, against the bridge. Then the issue would be fairly before the court. If the Attorney General can be persuaded that the General Government, by reason of anything in the Constitution, or in any legislation of Congress, commands in the waters of the Hudson, instead of the government of New York, in regard to what may, or may not, be deemed obstructions to the highway of that river, by works of public improvement and public accommodation, constructed under State authority; and if he can be persuaded that the proposed bridge will, if erected, be an unlawful obstruction, and a public nuisance and public crime, it will be his duty to proceed against it. In such a case, the Court would be relieved from all embarrassment, and all undue responsibility. The Wheeling bridge case is an example of the injustice which is done the Court, when it is asked to pronounce a bridge to be a public nuisance at the instance, and in the interest, of a private party, and when the public against which the offence bears, if there be any, is not consulted or represented before the Court. In that case, the decision of the Court that the bridge must be deemed a public nuisance, was reversed by the very extraordinary mode of a public law, passed for this purpose, by the very government against which the alleged nuisance was supposed to have been committed.

This is not the case of a nuisance, if a nuisance at all, such as a private trespasser may commit by placing unlawful obstructions in the highway of a road or a river. Our bridge is to be erected under color, at least, of sovereign authority, and is not to be treated as a naked trespass, growing into an act of public criminality. A State may err in the exercise of its sovereignty, but it cannot commit a crime or a misdemeanor. This bridge is not a public offence against the State, or the public of the State. It is not a *purpresture* by the laws of the State. A *purpresture* is an unauthorized encroachment on the property or soil of the sovereign, in a highway, river or harbor. (Per Ch. Kent, in Attorney General v. Utica Insurance Company, 2 J. Ch. R., p. 381.) The soil of the Hudson river, out of all question, is the property of the State, and the State could not commit a *purpresture* on its own property. If it is a nuisance of this particular kind, called a *purpresture*, as against the government of the United States, then it is so because the United States owns, or is the sovereign over, the soil of the Hudson river, and not the State of New York, and because the bridge will be an unlawful obstruction to *their* river. If the United States do not own the soil of the Hudson river, then whatever else the bridge may be, it is not a nuisance of the kind called *purpresture*. It would be difficult to maintain that a State could commit a nuisance of any kind against the United States; but if, by reason of the supremacy of the National Government in particular things, the erection of this bridge, though authorized by the State, would be an unlawful obstruction to a public river where that government commands, and hostile to the constitution and laws of that government, and, in this sense, something to be called a public nuisance; if this be all so, there is no reason why the Court should, but every reason why it should not, entertain a suit and motion to put down the supposed nuisance at the instance, and solely in the interest, of a private party, who has an adequate remedy at law for his private injury, if he sustains any. Certainly it would be safer to wait for the proper law officer of the government, whose business it is to take care of the public interests in this regard, if there be, or is likely to be, any such nuisance as is charged, to complain of the bridge, and ask the Court to apply the proper corrective.

VI.

The question whether the bridge in this case will, if erected, be a public nuisance, assuming now that the Court can and will entertain that question on these Bills of complaint, turns, of course, on the point whether it will create an unlawful obstruction to that free navigation of the river to which the public are supposed to be entitled, and which the complainants insist is secured to the public by the Constitution and the legislation of Congress.

Allowing then, to the Act for granting licenses for the Coasting trade, and to the licenses granted under it, all the authority and effect which can be claimed for them as conferring a personal right on all who hold them, to the free navigation of the Hudson river, and of all the rivers and public waters of the United States, the question now to be considered is, will the proposed bridge, if erected as authorized and prescribed by the law of the State, so unlawfully obstruct the free navigation of the Hudson river as to amount to a public nuisance, and a public offence against the United States? I admit, in this connection, that whatever may be the right of the complainants under their licenses, the same right of free navigation belongs, or may belong, to the whole people of the United States. The question here presented necessarily involves the consideration of a supposed conflict between the authority and laws of the two governments, State and National.

Certain points of doctrine in regard to repugnancy and conflict, are deemed to be too well settled in this Court, to require that anything more should be done than to state them. The power of Congress "to regulate commerce with foreign nations, and among the several states," is an exclusive power; but the power is dormant until Congress legislates in execution of it. A measure adopted under State authority, and under an acknowledged power, which may affect commerce in some particular wherein Congress has the power to legislate but has not done so, would not be an unconstitutional act on the part of the State. To make repugnance or a conflict in such a case there must be something more than the mere delegation of the power over commerce to Congress; there must be Congressional legislation covering the subject. (Gibbons v. Ogden, 9 Wheat. R. 240, and Willson v. Blackbird Creek Marsh Co., 8 Curtis 105.)

There is no direct repugnance to the constitutional provision which clothes Congress with the power over commerce, in the measure which the legislation of the State has authorized in this case. If this legislation, however, is so in conflict with any act of Congress passed to regulate commerce, that the legislation of both governments cannot stand, as a practical thing, but one or the other must give way, then that of the State must yield. This conflict of laws, if practically developed in an irreconcilable conflict of measures, or of rights, under such laws respectively, makes the State legislation inoperative under the provisions of the Constitution.

Now the complainants claim that Congress has legislated under its power to regulate commerce, in the Act which provides for the licensing of vessels for the Coasting trade, and that they are armed with the authority of licenses under that Act, and are thus entitled, as are all persons armed with the same authority, by the express legislation of Congress, to the free navigation of the Hudson. They add, that that right of free navigation extends up the river to Troy, because Congress has made Troy a port of delivery.

Taking the right then, as here stated, will the proposed bridge, if erected as authorized, so materially obstruct the navigation of the river that the reasonable right of the complainants, and others, to the free navigation, as claimed to be secured to them under their licenses, cannot be enjoyed, but will be unreasonably interrupted and injured by the effect of the bridge? Is there anything in the allegations and proofs before the Court to authorize it so to pronounce and declare?

The complainants do not, as I understand them, go the extravagant length of maintaining that their licenses give them an absolute and unrestricted right to enter the waters of New York free from any question, impediment, hindrance or delay, by or under the authority of the State; or to sail their vessels on the waters of the Hudson river, in the channels, or along the shores, wherever there was water enough to float them at the date of their licenses, or at the date of the Act under which the licenses were granted, free from any obstruction, hindrance or difficulty of any kind, however slight, created by, or under the authority, of the State.

It is more than three-quarters of a century since the Act for granting licenses for the coasting trade was passed, and during all that time vessels licensed for that trade have been navigating the Hudson river. Within that period the State has done, or authorized, a great many things which have affected the navigation. Wharves and piers, carried far into the river from its original shores, have been constructed at New York, and Albany, and various other places. Nobody has ever complained of these, and they are not now complained of. Every one of these constructions is an encroachment, to a greater or less extent, on the free, natural flow of the river, and on the full freedom of navigation upon it in its natural state. Ferries are established across the river at various places under State authority. There are four steam ferry boats in almost constant motion at Albany. And every ferry boat on the river is in some degree an impediment to free navigation. A bridge exists at Troy, below the flow of the tide, which can only be passed by a narrow draw. A dam exists higher up, but still below the flow of the tide, which can only be passed by locks. All these are obstructions or impediments to free navigation, existing by State authority, and are not complained of. Throughout the United States, in all the navigable waters, the like obstructions and impediments have been created by State authority, and seldom, if ever, questioned. The State has a Quarantine establishment, standing guard perpetually over the entrance into its waters, and there foreign vessels, and vessels of the United States, both of the military and mercantile marine, are arrested and detained for hours, days or weeks, as a sanitary measure, at the pleasure of the State, and solely under State authority. If Mr. Frederick W. Coleman should come along with his coasting schooner, the Vintage, from Barnstable, in Massachusetts, and should come to this Quarantine ground with a pestilence on board, his vessel would be arrested until he could get permission from State authority to pursue his voyage up the Hudson river. Here is a liability to a more serious interruption to the perfectly free use of the navigable waters of the State, to a longer delay, and to heavier loss and damage, than any ever likely to arise from any bridge over the Hudson. But nobody doubts, the complainants do not doubt, the right of the State to interfere thus far, and in this manner, with the rights of free navigation, as claimed to be secured by the legislation of Congress, under the power to regulate commerce.

It cannot, then, be claimed by the complainants, that the rights of navigation in the Hudson river as secured to them by the legislation of Congress, and their licenses, are so absolute, that they are subject to no obstruction, impediment, delay, or restriction whatever, and no matter how inconsiderable, from the legislation and measures of the State. The legislation of Congress is paramount, and nothing in State legislation which directly and absolutely contravenes it, can stand. But much of the legislation of both governments may stand, notwithstanding a partial interference. The power to regulate commerce belongs to the General Government. That is one power. The power of police, under which quarantine and health laws are made, and the power to make roads and establish ferries and bridges, belong to the State. These are distinct and independent powers. They belonged to the State originally, when its sovereignty was absolute, and they were not taken away by the Constitution. If they are, in a certain sense and degree, subject to the power of Congress over commerce, yet the original powers remain, and are still powers of sovereignty. When these independent powers are exercised by the respective governments, partial interferences and collisions are liable to arise in the measures they may authorise, or in the rights they may protect. But such partial interferences and collisions do not make the laws of the respective governments so absolutely incompatible and repugnant, that they cannot stand together. Wherever the laws of both can have a fair and reasonable operation and effect, both must be maintained. Without this principle, it would be impossible to maintain our complex system, impossible to make it operate in harmony, and secure the immense advantages which our daily experience shows us flow from the wise and beneficent adjustment of the powers of government in our State and National organizations. It has been the fixed policy of the country to maintain the principle to which I have referred. Congress adopts the pilot laws of the States, even while the power of the States to pass such laws is doubted. Congress passes laws to encourage and aid in the full execution of the quarantine and health laws of the States, though these laws materially interfere with that freedom of navigation which is supposed to be secured to all vessels sailing under its authority. (Ch. J. Marshall's opinion in Gibbons vs. Ogden.) Congress adopts the roads of the States for its post-roads, and for its military roads, though the power to make such roads for itself can hardly be doubted.

The question between the proposed bridge in our case, and the rights of free navigation supposed to be secured by the authority of Congress, must stand on this same principle and policy. Will the bridge be such an obstruction that the law of Congress in reference to licenses, giving it, in general terms, the construction which the complainants attribute to it, cannot have a fair and reasonable operation? Will it be such an obstruction that the rights of the complainants to the free navigation of the river, under licenses supposed to be intended to secure them from improper State interference, cannot be fairly and reasonably enjoyed? May not the bridge stand, as a measure of public improvement devised by the State, and all fair and reasonable rights of navigation still remain to the complainants and the public, substantially as claimed by them?

The river is not to be closed by the bridge; that cannot be pretended. The bridge is to be adapted to the position it is to occupy, with special reference to the preserving of open and unobstructed channels under and through it, for all the navigation that will have occasion to use them, or the river above. Eight-tenths of all that floats there will pass freely under the bridge at all stages of water. For the rest, it will have one draw of 180 feet in width, or two draws of 110 feet each. It requires no proof, it admits of no denial, that this provision is ample for the passage of the largest vessels navigating the river. It is a plain mathematical fact. The "Great Eastern" could pass through with ease, if there was water enough to float her. It is not a question whether the passage with the bridge will be as wide and ample as it is without it. It is not a question whether there may not, at times at least, be some little difficulty, some little inconvenience, some little detention, some little hazard even, in passing the bridge. Not only some little of all this, but a great deal of it all, is incident to the very nature of navigation, as well on rivers, as in bays and harbors, and on the open sea.

It seems clear that a vessel cannot move between Albany and Troy without encountering inconveniences quite as great as any to be met with in passing the proposed bridge. Tows, as they are called, some acres of craft spread broad and long over the river, and dragging their slow length along, often to the great annoyance of other vessels and interests of navigation, may not be able to pass the bridge without some temporary diminution and lowering of their huge proportions and pretensions. If they cannot pass in grand column, they may easily break ranks a little, and so pass. They have to do this in other parts of the river. Grand armies have to do the like in all their marches. The river was not made for tows alone, of the Leviathan order. Such things were not dreamed of when the license law of Congress was passed. They are entitled to all due consideration, but not to any monopoly of rights or accommodation on the river.

The true question is, will the bridge, instead of closing the highway of the river, leave a liberal and ample gateway for every thing that floats there? If it will, then we say there is no real collision, no incompatibility between the bridge, as a beneficent measure of public improvement under the authority of the State, and the rights of free navigation, as supposed to be secured under the authority of Congress. The complainants and the public may still navigate the highway of the river freely, while a noble highway athwart the river, equally demaded for the use of the public, is also secured. To complain, or talk of such a measure as a public nuisance, seems to me to pervert language, and heap contempt on truth and reason.

What is "free" navigation? We have seen that those who claim free navigation, are still forced to submit to some abatement of the idea of an absolute and unrestricted scope and verge for the sailing of their craft. Freedom of navigation is a thing not difficult to be understood. It is perfectly well defined in practice on European rivers, and the Publicists are not silent on the subject.

Vattel, when treating of the common right of navigating public rivers under the regulations of the sovereign, says:

"This right necessarily supposes that the river shall remain *free and navigable*, and therefore excludes every work that will *entirely* interrupt its navigation." (Vattel, Chitty's 7 Am. ed., pp. 123-4; B. I. sec. 273.)

The doctrine is that a river remains free and navigable, so long as its navigation is not *entirely* interrupted. Wharves and piers, and bridges with draws, do not entirely obstruct navigation, but leave the navigation open, and therefore free, in respect to physical obstructions.

When the navigation is thus left open, and is not embarrassed by oppressive duties and regulations, then it is free in the accepted European sense, and according to the doctrine of the Publicists. (1 Kent's Com., p. 35, 2d ed.)

In 1815, the European Powers, by the treaty of Paris, established the freedom of navigation on the Rhine, and made arrangements for extending the principle to other European rivers, which, like the Rhine, separated or traversed the territories of several States. The movement was made upon a Memoir of Baron William Von Humboldt, the Plenipotentiary of Prussia. A reference to the proceedings and papers will show that the freedom of navigation sought to be achieved, was the exemption from the various and vexatious commercial and custom-house regulations and impositions of the several riparian States, which had always greatly impeded navigation, and sometimes had shut up a river entirely. In the final act of the Congress of Vienna, it was declared that the navigation of these rivers should be "entirely free" ("*entière-*

ment libre ") and could not, in respect to commerce, be interdicted ("*interdite*") to any body. (Wheat. Hist. Law of Nations, pp. 498—504.)

Minute provisions were made for the regulation of commerce, and the imposition of duties, by laws of common obligation among the riparian States, leaving to these States respectively their rights of sovereignty in all other respects. No stipulations were made, or suggested, to restrain the several riparian States from physical obstructions to the navigation by means of bridges, or other necessary erections. Bridges then existed, and more exist now, over these rivers—many of them to be passed only by means of draws. No necessity was felt for any special provision on this subject. Besides that no apprehension could be entertained that any riparian State would wholly shut up the navigation and commerce of its own river by physical obstructions—which must always be an act of suicidal folly—the law of nations provided for the case, if it should ever occur. The impediment to navigation which constituted the whole danger and the whole evil, was the various and conflicting regulations, duties, and exactions which the several riparian States were at liberty to, and did, impose on the commerce and navigation of the rivers which were common to these States. When commerce and navigation were regulated by a law of common obligation to them all, then the navigation was "entirely free." It was assumed that the navigation would remain *open*, because, by the law of nations, no State could establish a work, be it a bridge or any other, which, in the language of Vattel, would "entirely interrupt navigation." Every riparian State would take care to leave the navigation open at least to its own citizens, and just as it was open to them, would it be open to the citizens of the other riparian States. A navigation thus open, and at the same time relieved from the impositions and exactions of particular States, and placed under a common law of commercial regulation, was an entirely "free" navigation in public law, and in common sense.

It is manifest that what was thus accomplished—after all, not in the most perfect manner—by the powers of Europe in 1815, in establishing freedom of navigation on their rivers, had been done in the most perfect and complete way, by the Constitution of the United States in 1787, in establishing freedom of navigation on all the navigable waters of the United States.

Before the Constitution, the same evils of separate and rival commercial regulations among the several States in this country had existed, as afflicted navigation and commerce on the European rivers, and it was exactly these evils that were sought to be, and were, effectually corrected and remedied by the provisions of the constitution. When the separate States had been forbidden to lay duties on imports or exports, or duties of tonnage, and the general regulation of commerce was confided to a common government, which all the States were bound to obey, and when, in addition to all this, it was provided that no State could give privileges and immunities to its own citizens to which the citizens of other States were not also entitled; when all this was done, freedom of navigation on all the navigable waters of the United States, was effectually and abundantly provided for. If, as the complainants here maintain, it belonged to Congress as a part of the power to regulate commerce, to provide by legislation against improper physical obstructions to navigation by the erection of wharves, piers, or bridges, under State authority or otherwise, and if Congress, as they maintain, has made that provision by its legislation in regard to licenses for the coasting trade, still the question remains, in respect to erections, made under State authority, in or over a navigable river, and which produce physical impediments to the navigation—when do they, and when do they not, leave the navigation open and free, in a proper and just legal signification? I know of no legal definition which the Court can apply to the subject but that which is derived from the law and the practice of nations. There can be no other safe rule. The law of free navigation in regard to physical obstructions in the rivers of the United States, created under State authority, still subject as such rivers are, confessedly, to the general sovereignty and jurisdiction of the several States within which they run, cannot be any other than that of the established law of nations. No other rule is adapted to the case. The Constitution provides no new rule on the subject; Congress has prescribed none; and surely this Court cannot make one.

The rule of the law of nations, in regard to physical obstructions, as I understand it, is, that if the navigation be left open to all who are entitled to use it, as it is to the citizens of the State making the erections, the navigation is free. If, for example, a low bridge is erected over a river by the sovereign entitled to make the erection, and the navigation is left fairly open by means of a draw, the navigation is free from any unlawful physical obstruction.

What constitutes then the full freedom of navigation of a river in this country, as all over the world, is, 1st, such freedom from physical obstruction as shall leave the navigation fairly open—as by a proper draw in a bridge; and next, freedom from such special legislation, exactions, impositions and regulations as separate riparian States might impose, and the subjection of the commerce and navigation to a common law of regulation, which all are bound to observe, so that all who are entitled to use the highway of the river enjoy equal rights and equal privileges in the navigation. This is what I understand constitutes in full, in all its length and breadth, that free navigation of the Hudson to which the complainants, and the public, are entitled.

It is the physical obstruction to the navigation which is complained of in this case. And the position I take on that point, is that, inasmuch as the proposed bridge will be constructed with a draw, or draws, which will leave the navigation open to all who are entitled to use it, the navigation is perfectly "free," in the legal acceptation of the term as applicable to all public rivers, and free, too, in the whole common sense of the subject.

It is sufficient if the navigation is left "open;" and nobody has a right to complain of any necessary restrictions which may attend this new condition of the navigation. Good faith requires that it should be left *fairly* open—a condition abundantly secured by the interest which the State itself has in a free navigation. In this case, there cannot be a doubt that the navigation is to be left, not only open, but fairly and liberally open, and in that sense, the only sense in which the complainants or the public have a right to demand it, entirely free.

I am glad to believe that the view I have now presented, of what free navigation is, in respect to physical obstructions authorized by State authority, is in perfect harmony with the opinions and decisions of the Courts of the United States, in all cases where complaints have been made before them against bridges over public rivers.

In the Cuyahoga Bridge Case, (3 McLean, R. 226,) Mr. Justice McLean said: "A dam may be thrown over the river provided a lock is so constructed as to permit boats to pass with little or no delay, and without charge." He said also in the same case: "A draw-bridge across a navigable river is not an obstruction."

The decision of the same learned judge in the Rock Island Bridge case, so far as he considered the question of obstruction, and the open navigation furnished by the draw, was in accordance with his opinion in the case just referred to.

In the Wheeling Bridge case, the majority of the Court held the bridge to be an unlawful obstruction, because it was an absolute impediment, because, in fact, in their judgment, it shut up the river at that point, to a certain class of vessels accustomed to use it—the class of steamers with tall chimneys. It was not provided with a draw. And Mr. Justice McLean, who delivered the opinion of the Court, said : " If the obstruction be slight, as a draw in a bridge, which would be safe and convenient for the passage of vessels, it would not be regarded as a nuisance, where proper attention is given to raise the draw on the approach of vessels." In the dissenting opinion in this case, of his Hon. the Chief Justice, it was wisely said, quite in accordance with the opinion just quoted: " Bridges have been erected over many navigable rivers, and built so near the water, that vessels can pass only through a draw. Such bridges are unquestionably obstructions, and impede navigation. For where the vessels are propelled by sails, and the wind is unfavorable, they are often detained not only for hours, but for days. The Courts of the United States have never exercised jurisdiction over any of these obstructions, nor declared them to be nuisances." It is only necessary to add in reference to this case, that the decree for abatement which had originally been made, was subsequently modified by the Court so as to authorize a draw to be constructed, such as, in the opinion of an engineer to whom the matter had been referred, would fairly open the navigation to the class of vessels to which otherwise the bridge was held to oppose an absolute obstruction. Such a draw was declared to be satisfactory, though vessels would be obliged to leave the principal and accustomed channel, and run an increased distance by another, to reach the draw.

These cases I think show a sufficient harmony with the doctrine which I have brought to the notice of the Court, with regard to physical obstructions under State authority in a navigable river. By this doctrine, when, as in this case, the Court sees that the State has made careful provision, by means of a draw in its proposed bridge, to keep the navigation fairly open, I think it is bound to assume that the draw will be sufficient for that purpose until at least the contrary is made to appear by practical demonstration after the erection is made. This I humbly think is the only convenient, the only safe, and the only legal course for the Court. But, at any rate, if the Court will entertain the question, and hear proofs in regard to the sufficiency of the draw before the erection is made, on a Bill in Equity by a private party, at least it should insist that the case against the sufficiency of the draw shall be made out with a certainty which shall leave nothing to doubt about.

The proposed bridge with a draw, authorized by the State, is *prima facie* a lawful bridge. It is not an obstruction by the test of the only rule of law which can be applied to the subject; it leaves the navigation fairly open and free. The opening will be ample, and the arrangements ample, to admit the easy passage of any vessel navigating the river. There will be a very wide draw, and comparatively a very narrow vessel to pass it. No testimony could impeach that broad fact. And with this fact alone I insist that the bridge is a lawful one. If delays and difficulties may occur, still they cannot impeach the lawfulness of the bridge, unless they are shown to be such as must amount to a practical impediment to the passing of the draw, so great that parties engaged in the navigation would be likely to abandon it as no longer free. No such difficulties or delays have been shown; none such can be shown in the nature of the case. The navigation will be fairly open, and therefore free—free in the sense of international law—free in any sense of the license law of Congress, which can be fairly attributed to it—free in the sense of the licenses granted under that law, even when taken, after the construction of the complainants, as a warrant of title in all who use them to the free navigation of the river.

VII.

But I come now to look at the case in another view. I hope I have shown that the proposed bridge will not be an unlawful erection and a nuisance, even if it be admitted that Congress, in the shape and guise of a regulation of commerce in respect to the coasting trade, has actually passed an Act, the object of which was to prevent and prohibit improper and undue obstructions by bridges, or other erections, in navigable rivers, and to control State legislation in relation to such erections. But I must now deny that Congress passed the Act for licensing vessels for the coasting trade, or that it has ever passed any Act, with the object and purpose thus attributed to it. I deny that there is any legislation of Congress of any kind, that purports to have any such object in view, or that can bear any such interpretation without an utter perversion of all the canons of interpretation usually applied to statutes.

In the Wheeling Bridge Case, certain general legislation of Congress for the regulation of commerce on all the navigable waters of the United States, in "licensing vessels, establishing ports of entry, imposing duties upon masters and other officers of boats, &c.," and also the sanction by Congress of the compact between Virginia and Kentucky, for the free navigation of the Ohio, were referred to by the Court as sufficient to warrant the Court in declaring the bridge as built, to be an obstruction, and a public nuisance.

But the Court can only administer the laws of the United States, not make them, or supply any defects in them. The question is, has Congress declared a bridge over a public river, or any erection of the sort, producing an impediment to navigation, to be an obstruction, and a public nuisance. If it has, the Court may administer that law by so pronouncing; if it has not, there is no law on the subject for the Court to administer.

Nothing, it seems to me, can be clearer than that Congress has adopted no system of legislation, and no Act of legislation, to prohibit or prevent obstructions in navigable waters. It has adopted no legislation which indicates any such object. No Act could have ever have been passed for such a purpose without eliciting debate, or without arousing attention, and, I may add, without the strongest opposition. There cannot be a doubt that the States are perfectly competent, and always perfectly ready, to prevent and punish any unauthorized obstructions in the navigable waters within their respective limits. As for the States themselves obstructing their own navigable waters, in any way to be a fit subject of complaint by their own citizens, by other States, or the citizens of other States, they no more need the guardianship of Congress, or of the Courts of the United States, to prevent such mischief, than they do to restrain them from breaking up their roads and railways, and filling up their canals, or setting fire to their own capitals, or burning up their own commercial cities. If Congress had ever legislated on such a subject as this, everybody would know it; the legislation would be plain and palpable, and the Courts would not have been left to grope in the dark after the law.

The laws passed by Congress for the regulation of commerce are in no sense laws to prohibit or prevent obstructions to navigable waters. They do not express, or indicate, any such purpose, and they are, in no particular or degree, adapted to meet and cover such an object. They are general regulations, attending vessels wherever they go on the navigable waters of the United States, and into whatever ports they enter.

A license for the coasting trade is an authority to a vessel to visit any waters of the United States which it may find open and navigable, and any port of entry or delivery, or any port not one of entry or delivery, which it may find accessible. But it is no pledge to the owner or navigator of the vessel, to go before him to clear away any obstructions he may meet with. The act for granting licenses is not an act to prohibit or prevent obstructions, or to declare an obstruction a public nuisance, and make provisions for the proper abatement and punishment of such a public offence.

It seems to me there was still less in the compact between Virginia and Kentucky, and the sanction of it by Congress (if it was so sanctioned,) which could be construed, or tortured even, into a law of Congress to prohibit obstructions in the Ohio, and declare them a public nuisance.

Under the Constitution, all the navigable rivers of the United States, those in the west as well as others, are free rivers to all the citizens of the United States. The compact in the Ordinance of 1787, which was before the Constitution, and the compact between Virginia and Kentucky, do not make the western rivers more free than the Constitution makes them, by various special provisions in relation to duties, navigation and commerce, and by declaring that the privileges and immunities of the citizens of each State shall be common to the citizens of all the States. All highways, whether of water or on land, which are common to the public of a State, are common to the public of the United States. The easement of a navigable river is for the use and enjoyment of the whole people. The whole design of the compacts referred to was to secure this very advantage, which is now so effectually secured everywhere by the Constitution. The whole object was, not to prevent physical obstructions in a river by the authority of a State, which no State could make or authorize without doing itself and its own citizens more harm than anybody else, but that the citizens of other States should be put on an exact equality with the citizens of the State within which a river might run, in regard to the use and enjoyment of the easement of such river. (Opinion of Ch. J. Taney in Wheeling Bridge case, 19 Curtis, p. 649.) The Constitution now secures this object perfectly. No State within which a navigable river runs, can impose any burthens, any disabilities, any restrictions or conditions upon the vessels or citizens of other states in using the easement of that river, that are not equally imposed upon the vessels and citizens of that State. Any State legislation in violation of this rule, would be repugnant to the Constitution, and the remedy and correction could be easily applied.

All the regulations of commerce by Congress are framed with a steady regard to exactly this state of things. They are general rules, and generally of universal application. They secure the perfect equality of all vessels, and of all citizens of whatsoever States, on the navigable rivers of every State. A coasting license secures exactly this equality, and that is all it secures. It certifies to its possessor, if a citizen of another State, a perfect equality of rights in the navigation of any river, which that river affords, under the sovereignty and jurisdiction of the State in which it runs, to the citizens of that State. Beyond that it has no meaning, and no force, in respect to freedom of navigation. Congress has been content thus far, and I believe it will always be content, to leave the sovereignty and jurisdiction of the several States, and the general police of their own rivers, in regard to obstructions therein, untouched and unrestricted. And to construe the Act providing for coasting licenses, or Acts establishing ports of entry or delivery, as laws assuming Federal jurisdiction over all navigable rivers, and as enactments to prohibit obstructions and declare them a public nuisance; this I must hold to be a perversion of the plain intent and meaning of statute law, such as has no parallel with which I am acquainted.

I do not see why the decision in the case of the Blackbird Creek Marsh Company, does not entirely cover the position that Congress has passed no law the object of which has been to control State legislation in regard to bridges and other erections in navigable waters. There a close dam had been made across a navigable creek by State authority. And in a suit which involved the consideration of all the authority that could be given to a license for the Coasting trade, the Court held that Congress had not legislated in a way to control the State in this act of sovereign power.

VIII.

I have one other view of this case to present to the Court. I have considered the case on the assumption that Congress has legislated in a manner, and with the intent, to control State legislation on the subject of erections in, or over, the navigable waters of the United States. I have next shown, or endeavored to show, that Congress has not legislated with any such intent, or to any such effect. I come now, finally, to a question which lies entirely back of these, and of all other questions in the case—a question fairly arising in the case, one which it is quite time this Court should consider and decide; and the decision of which, in accordance with the view which I entertain of it, would not only dispose of the whole issue between these parties, whatever might be the opinion of the Court on the other points raised and discussed in the suit, but would settle and quiet forever the whole disturbing subject, now so fruitful of litigation, of a supposed conflict between the National and State governments in regard to an important branch of sovereignty and jurisdiction over the waters of the United States.

The question which I have to present and discuss, is this: Has Congress, under the power " to regulate commerce with foreign nations, and among the several States," authority to pass laws to prohibit, or to remove, what it may deem obstructions to navigation, in the navigable waters of the United States, by erections therein, under State authority, exercised within the territorial limits of the States respectively; or to prescribe terms and conditions on which such erections may be made, or to regulate the same; and by such Congressional legislation to control or restrict State legislation on the subject.

In other words, the question is, may the National Government, by its legislation under the commercial power, oust the States of their sovereignty and jurisdiction over the navigable waters within their limits respectively, and itself assume jurisdiction so far as to command exclusively, in and over the same, and over the soil under the waters, in whatsoever may concern or affect the easement or freedom of navigation therein, due to the public; exercising all the powers of sovereignty over all the navigable waters of the United States, and over the land under these waters, which any sovereign can exercise over the navigable waters, and the land under them, within his own dominions?

I am perfectly aware that the power of Congress, which I here propose to dispute, has generally been assumed and taken for granted, in the Courts of the United States, without question or discussion. It has, however, only been assumed in the *dicta* of the Courts in delivering opinions. No case, so far as I am aware, can be deemed to have been made to turn or stand on this assumed power, possibly with the exception of the Wheeling Bridge Case; and there the question was not raised and discussed at the bar, or considered and decided by the Court. The power was merely assumed, and thus alluded to in argument. I hope, under all the circumstances, and considering the immense importance of the question, the Court will not think we are too late in raising that question now, and asking for a solemn decision upon it.

All navigable waters within the State, such as the common law calls navigable, are a part of the domain of the States in which they lie. A State owns the soil and bed of its navigable waters as far as the tide flows. Its jurisdiction over them is that of a sovereign. Its civil power over them is that of a sovereign. Navigable waters, within the dominions of a sovereign, are the property of the sovereign; the public, however, under the sovereign, has a right to the easement upon them for navigation.

But the sovereign may make grants therein, interfering in some measure, with the navigation,—as for fisheries and the like. The sovereign may even close the navigation for strong reasons of State ; as for sanitary purposes, or where public policy demands it. The case of the Blackbird Creek Marsh Company is an example. The right of the public to navigate a navigable river, is perfect as against all private and unauthorized obstructions. But the sovereign may, for reasons of State, create impediments to the navigation, and no subject or citizen has a right to complain of it, or can bring any action for injury to the rights of navigation, or injuries to property affected thereby. It is presumed the sovereign has good reason for the measures he may adopt, and if remote incidental damages follow from them, the citizen has no remedy but by petition to the sovereign. If the sovereign takes away his property by any public act, he must make compensation for it. These are general and familiar principles which need only to be stated to the Court, to receive its full recognition.

All this sovereignty and right belonged to every State in reference to its navigable waters, before the Constitution. The sovereignty was not taken away by any express provision in the Constitution, and transferred to the National Government. That Government is not declared to be the sovereign of any part of the proper domain of a State, whether it is land or water, or land under water.

It is true, Congress is clothed with power to regulate commerce, and it becomes a material question, how far Congress, by its legislation under this power, may control State legislation in the exercise of that sovereignty I have just been describing. The conferring of such a power does not take the sovereignty and domain from the State, and bestow it on the National Government. It does not affect the sovereignty until some legislation takes place in execution of the power; and what Congress may do, and what it may not do, in execution of this power, we must endeavor to ascertain and define. If it had been intended to transfer State sovereignty, over all the territory of the States covered by navigable waters, constituting so large a part of their domain, to the National Government, it would have been done with at least as much formality and explicitness as was observed in conferring exclusive government upon Congress, over the seat of the National Government, and over the places where its forts and other needful buildings are established.

I have already had occasion to show that the grant of Admiralty and Maritime jurisdiction does not affect the proper sovereignty of the State. It does not carry a cession of the waters, where these cases may arise, or the general jurisdiction over them.

It does not admit of a doubt, as I suppose, that the sovereignty and general jurisdiction over the navigable waters, within the boundaries of a State, remain with the State. The question then arises, how far may the legislation of the State, in execution of this sovereignty and general jurisdiction, be controlled by the legislation of Congress under the power to regulate commerce? Does this power authorize Congress to assume that sovereignty over the territory covered by the navigable waters of a State, which the National Government must exercise, exclusive of the State, if it is to command in and over the waters, in whatsoever may affect the condition, for practical use, of the easement therein, to which the public are entitled?

The power to regulate commerce is exclusive, to whatever extent it may be rightfully exercised by Congress. No State can exercise it, or any part of it. Whatever is, or may be a regulation of commerce, must be effected by

National legislation. And commerce includes navigation and intercourse. It is not confined to water, and places accessible by water. It passes inland, and moves on the soil, and inland waters, among the States. The power of Congress attends foreign and inter-state commerce, wherever it goes, for all necessary purposes of legal regulation; and this power is the same on the land as on the water. Whatever Congress may do in control of State legislation and State sovereignty on the navigable waters within a State, it may do on the land, wherever routes of foreign or inter-state commerce are, or may be established.

The history of commerce under the Confederation, reveals very clearly the mischiefs of independent State regulation, which were intended to be remedied by making the general commerce of the country national, and making one government responsible for its regulation. Commercial treaties could not be made or maintained, without this national power over foreign commerce. Without it, the foreign commerce and navigation of the country were under the sway of foreign powers. The whole navigating interest of the United States was liable to be sacrificed to the foreign navigating interest engaged in American commerce. Even that engaged in the coasting trade, and in the fisheries, was liable to the same disability and sacrifice, and hence the necessity of making the national power over commerce cover the trade between the States, a necessity made imperative by the interested, oppressive, and retaliatory legislation, between individual States, or classes of States, affecting most injuriously; not only the foreign and coastwise trade, but the internal trade between the States.

Much of the original mischief was directly met and prevented, by specific provisions in the Constitution. Congress cannot tax the exports from any State; nor abuse its power by giving the ports of one State preference over those of another; or by requiring vessels bound to or from one State to enter, clear or pay duties, in another; or by laying any duties, imposts, or excises, but such as are uniform throughout the United States. And an effectual restriction is laid upon the States to prevent their laying duties on imports or exports, or duties of tonnage. Nor can a State confer any privileges or immunities in respect to commerce within the State, on its citizens, which will not equally belong to the citizens of other States.

For the rest, the regulation of commerce is left to the legislation of Congress. By the legislation of Congress, an American commercial marine is established, and a national character impressed upon the vessels and crews engaged in commerce; the shipping interest in the foreign trade is protected against injurious foreign legislation, or decrees; the coasting trade is secured to the home interest in shipping and navigation; convenient ports of entry and delivery are established, and custom house officers appointed to conduct the necessary business at such ports; vessels engaged in commerce are furnished with papers which fix their character and privileges, and coasting vessels receive a license from year to year, which is their warrant and authority to pass from port to port, wherever they find ports accessible, and to navigate the waters of the United States, wherever they find the waters navigable.

We all know that in the original movements, which resulted in establishing a new government, commerce was the chief thing considered. In the instructions to most of the delegates who met at Annapolis, the main thing required was, to enquire how far a *uniform system* in the commercial intercourse and regulations of the United States was necessary.

In the Constitutional Convention, in committee of the whole, on the several plans for forming a new government, the rule adopted as to specific powers to be given to Congress, was, that it should legislate in those cases " to which the States were separately incompetent, or in which the harmony of the States would be interrupted by the exercise of individual legislation." This rule applies to this commercial power as conferred by the Constitution. All the legislation of Congress which comes properly and directly under the head of this power, will be found to have had a general reference to the rule which confines such legislation to doing what the States are separately incompetent to do, or what, if attempted by them, would interrupt their harmony.

Without touching the question of disputed right, whether Congress has, or has not, authority to protect and encourage domestic industry, under the power to regulate commerce, I may remark, that the form of affecting the object, whenever duties have been laid *primarily* for protection, is strictly one of commercial regulation; that as a commercial regulation it is one to which the separate States are clearly incompetent, and one in which, if attempted, (as certainly it could not be) the harmony of the States would be necessarily interrupted by individual legislation.

But Congress has done many things, and the authority of Congress to do many other things is often claimed, which have some manifest relation to commerce ; and the question is, where does Congress get the power to do them ? Congress establishes and maintains light-houses, buoys, beacons and breakwaters, and has at times engaged in removing natural obstructions from bays, sounds and rivers. It has prosecuted for a series of years, and still prosecutes, at great cost, that most beneficent and magnificent work, the Coast Survey. Under what power is all this done? Not, certainly, as a direct exercise of the power to regulate commerce. A light-house, a buoy, or a breakwater is certainly not a regulation of commerce. Nor is the removal of a rock, or a sand bar, in navigable waters, a regulation of commerce. They aid commerce, but do not regulate it. They are a means of facilitating and carrying on commerce. But Congress has no direct authority to carry on commerce, or to supply the means of carrying it on, but only to regulate it as carried on. Nor can these measures properly come under the "incidental" power—that of making laws "for carrying into execution" the power to regulate commerce. They are not means " necessary and proper" for carrying any regulation of commerce into execution. They are not adapted to such an object. A regulation for the government of seamen on board of American ships ; for conferring privileges on ships built and owned in the United States ; for laying discriminating or countervailing duties; for granting licenses for the coasting trade or fisheries ; such regulations of commerce are not carried, or aided in being carried, into execution by any of the measures just referred to. They may, and do, tend to protect, increase, multiply and facilitate commerce as and where it is carried on ; but the execution of every act of commercial regulation is just as perfect without as with them.

If these measures are to be justified under any "incidental" power, it is rather under that of making laws for carrying into execution the power of Congress to lay and collect duties on imports ; that is, the taxing power. As Congress is authorized to raise revenue by duties on imports, it might, with plausibility at least, be argued that to carry into execution this power in a way to produce the required revenue at the least burthen, it is necessary and proper that measures should be adopted to increase, multiply, facilitate and protect commerce in all practicable ways, and that these measures are fitted and adapted to that object.

But the true constitutional ground on which these measures stand, is that of the direct and substantive power of Congress to make appropriations for such objects, of a national character, as are " for the common defence and the general welfare of the United States." This is taking the most natural and safe construction of this power, namely, that it is a power of taxation, but limited to objects and uses of a national character. The power to lay taxes, taken as an independent power, and subject to no restriction, would have been absolute and arbitrary, and Congress might have raised revenue and applied it to any purpose it might choose. But when the objects of raising revenue are especially limited to those of " paying the debts, and providing for the common defence and general welfare of the United States," taxation is limited and restrained, and the proceeds can only be applied to purposes of a *general and national* character within the purview of the Constitution. (Story's Com. Ch. 14.)

On no other just ground than this, can appropriations to make, or aid in making, internal improvements in roads, harbors, and rivers rest. Appropriations for lighthouses, buoys, and breakwaters, for the Coast Survey, and for all the indispensable aids to the national commerce, rest properly, on the same firm foundation. I am not of the number of those who deny the power of Congress to appropriate money for the improvement of harbors and rivers. I think it has not done half as much of this sort of work as it ought to have done. But I do not find the authority for it in the commercial power. Whenever such an improvement is national in its character, object, and importance, appropriations for it have an abundant warrant in that direct power which I have named. It is under this power, and not the commercial power, that Congress formerly made appropriations for the improvement of the navigation of the Hudson river above and below Albany; and I think the general interests of commerce, and of the country, would have been greatly advanced if that policy had been duly prosecuted, instead of being virtually abandoned, as it was many years ago.

Here then, as I venture to think, is the legitimate and true constitutional ground on which appropriations for the class of objects just referred to rest, and the question before the Court is not embarrassed by any necessity of assuming, or supposing, that they have been made, and could only be made, under the power to regulate commerce, or the power *incident* thereto, as being "necessary and proper" to carry that power into execution.

There is nothing in the action of Congress authorizing these measures; nothing in their history; nothing in the Constitution, requiring or, as I think, authorizing the Court to set them down to the account of the commercial power.

There is nothing in the Constitution which places the jurisdiction of the waters of a State, in regard to the easement of the public therein for navigation, in the hands of the National Government, any more than it places the jurisdiction of the land, and soil of the State, in the same hands, in regard to the easement of the common roads and highways in it, when they are routes and highways of foreign or inter-state commerce. So far as the waters are navigable, and the easement remains dedicated to the use of the people of the State, they are equally open and free to the citizens of all the other States; and just in the same manner, the roads of the State are open and free to the use of all, because "the citizens of each State shall be entitled to all the privileges and immunities of citizens in the several States."

In all this respect, there is no difference between the land and the water. The roads, railways and canals of a State are no more under the sovereignty and jurisdiction of the State, than are its navigable waters; and State legislation over the navigable waters of the State, in respect to their condition as highways of general commerce, is no more subject to be controlled by the paramount legislation of Congress, than is State legislation over its roads, railways and canals, where they are highways of the like commerce.

If the power to regulate commerce, or the power incident thereto, authorizes Congress by its legislation, to establish the supremacy of the National Government over the waters of a State, in all that concerns or affects their navigableness, it authorizes Congress also, and equally, to establish its supremacy over the main avenues and routes, in and through the land of the State, so far as they are, or can be made, the channels or highways of foreign commerce, or commerce between State and State. If Congress has authority, by the commercial power, to take the Hudson river under its sovereignty and jurisdiction, because it is a highway of commerce between the States, and can forbid any erections to be placed therein, by State authority, or any but such as Congress shall prescribe, it has the same authority to construct a road, a railway, or a canal through the State, between the Hudson river and Canada on the north, or Lake Erie and the States bordering thereon, and still further on in the west, and to exercise sovereignty and jurisdiction over such road, railway or canal, as highways of commerce, and forbid all erections in or over them by State authority, or all but such as itself shall prescribe. This precise power has been claimed for Congress as a commercial power. (Story's Com. Ab., p. 454, sec. 633 ; orig. sec. 1269)

According to this doctrine, Congress itself might have made the Erie and Champlain canals, as highways of foreign commerce, and commerce between State and State, with ports of entry or delivery at the termini; artificial rivers, the jurisdiction and control of which, for all the uses of commerce, would have belonged to the National government, with authority to keep the hands of the State government off from them, allowing no erections in or over them, not even a bridge, out of the many hundreds now thrown over them, but such as Congress might allow and prescribe. On the same principle Congress might have constructed the trunk or main lines of our railways, leading from the great commercial center of the State, to their northern and western connections with a foreign country, and with other States, and might have controlled them, as highways of commerce, against all interference of State authority.

Congress might go further. The railways and canals of New York, are as much highways of commerce, for foreign trade, and that between States, as the Hudson river, or any other river, or water in the whole Union. The trade between the United States and Canada through these channels, amounts to many millions annually ; and that between the States to many times as many millions more. If Congress, under the commercial power, has a right to command in the channels and highways of foreign and inter-State commerce, for the protection of such commerce, by its paramount authority, as against State interference or control in the matter of physical obstructions,—then on principle, there is no reason why the National Government should not assume the sovereign command on the railways and canals of New York, constructed by the State, as well as on the Hudson river, for the protection of the foreign and inter-state commerce therein, against State interference. It might legislate not only to make regulations for this commerce, by establishing ports of entry or delivery, along the line and at the termini of these routes, and by granting licenses of passage and navigation as in the coasting trade, but to prescribe and control the construction of all locks and bridges on the canals, and of all the viaducts and crossings of the railways, and of their gauge and grades. The right of the State to take tolls and fares, in consideration of the cost of these works, would probably be respected.

The internal commerce of the country is many times greater than the foreign commerce; and that part of it which is properly foreign and inter-state commerce, taking carriage and travel together, moving on the land, by way of the roads, railways and canals, can hardly be less than that moving on the rivers of the United States. If it is necessary and proper that Congress should assume the paramount jurisdiction over these rivers, so far as to control and direct all erections in or over them, and whatever else might affect their navigableness, it would seem to be equally necessary and proper that it should extend the like paramount jurisdiction over the land, so far as to control and direct all structures in or over the roads, railways and canals, used for foreign and inter-state commerce, and whatever else might affect their availability or utility, as the highways of such commerce. It would not be easy, I think, to find one reason, founded in principle, necessity, or propriety, and having reference to the power to regulate commerce, why Congress should exercise that sort of paramount jurisdiction which I have described, over the navigable waters of the several States, which does not equally require and demand, that it should exercise the same kind of jurisdiction over the land, wherever great routes for foreign and inter-state commerce are, or may be established.

The fact that some of these waters of the States, flow into the ocean, and that the ocean flows into them by its tides, or the fact that some of them flow through, or between two or more States, cannot affect the general doctrine respecting this jurisdiction. The Constitution leaves these waters where it leaves the land, under the general sovereignty of the States. If in giving to Congress the power to regulate commerce, it authorizes that body to assume this particular jurisdiction over the waters, it must give it the same jurisdiction over the highways of general commerce on the land, for precisely the same object and under the same necessity. There is nothing in the nature of the power, or in the nature of the subject, to mark a distinction between the two cases. All that can be said about it is, that it might be a little less difficult for Congress to assert this jurisdiction on the waters than on the land.

The fact that these waters are natural highways, while roads, railways and canals, are highways of artificial construction, cannot affect the question before us. It is a question of sovereignty and jurisdiction, to be exercised for a specific object,—that of protecting commerce whereever it moves, on the water or on the land. If this is a necessary jurisdiction in the general government, on the water, it is necessary also on the land. If it is necessary in order to keep open and free, highways of commerce on the water, as against State interference, it is equally necessary, in order to keep open and free, highways of commerce on the land, as against State interference. The same motive, and the same interest, if any such can be conceived, which would lead a State to obstruct commerce on the waters under its jurisdiction, would lead it to obstruct commerce on the land. There can be no doubt, I suppose, that, before the Constitution, any State might have shut up its navigable rivers, flowing wholly within its own limits, from the use of the citizens of other States, or admitted them on its own terms. It cannot now do this, except by closing them to its own citizens; an authority which it is safe to say can never be exercised over a river of any public importance. This authority does not differ in kind, and hardly in degree, from that which a State exercises over its roads, railways, and canals. They are highways for public use, subject to the general sovereignty of the State.

The change which the Constitution wrought in respect to navigable waters, was: First, that the navigable waters of every State, should be as free to the citizens of all other States, as to its own;—and next, that so far as they should remain free and open to its own citizens, being free and open to all the citizens of the United States, the navigation and commerce upon them (except that which might be purely domestic to the State) should be subject to the regulation of Congress. The Constitution wrougth the same change on the land. The highways of a State must be as free to the citizens of other States as to its own; and so far as they are free and open to its own citizens, being also free and open to all other citizens of the United States, whatever of foreign or inter-State commerce moves upon them, is subject to the regulation of Congress. In both cases, and equally, the sovereignty and jurisdiction otherwise remain with the State. It was no part of the purpose of the Constitution, under the power to regulate commerce, to clothe Congress with authority to assume the sovereignty over the channels and highways of commerce, within the several States, whether by water or land, to the exclusion of the States, in respect to whatever might concern or affect their condition and availability for the uses of commerce. That was a matter which belonged to the States, and was properly left to their control. It devolved on the General government to give uniformity and freedom to commerce, by its regulations, wherever that commerce, under individual enterprise and conduct, should find open and free highways for itself among the States, whether on the water or on the land, leaving those highways, and all that might affect their condition and availability as such, to the jurisdiction, control and care of the States.

The channels and highways of commerce in the States, wherever open, being made free to all the citizens of the United States, by express provisions of the Constitution, it remained only to make the commerce itself free—free from all partial and conflicting legislation of the States—and to give it a national character by such uniform regulations as Congress alone could make.

Happily, we have now the experience of seventy years to show the wisdom of this arrangement. The States have exercised this jurisdiction and control, almost without question, from the foundation of the government. They have never asked the leave of the General government to make any erections in or over their waters which they might see fit to make, any more than to make and govern their own roads, railways and canals on the land. In one instance only (that of the Wheeling bridge), has that Government, by any department of it, interposed to take this jurisdiction out of the hands of a State, or to dictate the terms on which it should be exercised. And in that case, the legislative department of the government came, in the end, to the relief of the State, by a public Act, sanctioning, so far as Congress could sanction, the exercise of State sovereignty on the subject. The result in that case has shown too, that the apprehensions of great and irreparable injury, whether to individuals, or to another State, from the exercise of this kind of sovereignty by a State over its own waters, were unfounded, since scarcely an appreciable injury, I believe, has been felt by anybody, from the Wheeling bridge, and nothing in comparison of the vast public benefit of the work. From the origin of the government, the States have gone on, in the exercise of their proper jurisdiction over their navigable waters, constructing or authorizing piers, wharves and bridges, all of them, in some sense and degree, encroachments on the channels and highways of navigation, as they originally existed. In some instances, the accustomed channels of navigable waters have been closed, or changed, by dams, through which navigation can only pass by means of locks. In the Cuyahoga bridge case, Mr. Justice McLean declared that this was a proper exercise of State authority. And where a navigable creek was wholly closed by a dam, the act of the State received the sanction of the Supreme Court. It did so in the case of the Blackbird Creek Marsh Company.

And thus far in the history of the country not a case has occurred, so far as I know, where this jurisdiction in the States has been abused, or in any manner employed to create unnecessary, improper or injurious obstructions to navigation in its own navigable waters. To admit the supposition that a State could be found capable of such wickedness or such reckless folly, would be to assume that such State is unfit, from moral degradation, to be a government at all, or to legislate for the affairs and interests of its own people.

That there shall be rivalries between States to secure each to itself the great currents of trade and travel between distant points of great commercial importance, is to be expected. But in these cases each will look to attain success, not by obstructing, but by improving and facilitating navigation, and the means of transit through its own territory. And if a State draws to itself advantages in this respect over another State, by its superior systems of internal improvement, or its superior natural position, the public interests at large are not injured by it, and the rival State has no right to complain.

The distinction between the jurisdiction which a State properly exercises over its own waters, and the jurisdiction over commerce which belongs to the General Government, is a broad and palpable one. What are regulations of commerce in order to make commerce free, is easily understood. The object has been accomplished in this country by special provisions in the Constitution, and by the legislation of Congress, which takes from the States all power to restrict, annoy or burthen commerce by partial and conflicting measures, affecting the objects or subjects of commerce, or the vessels or agencies employed in transportation and carriage.

The regulations adopted by the European powers to secure the freedom of commerce on the Rhine, and other rivers, were of the same character as those contemplated by the Constitution to secure the freedom of commerce on the waters of the United States. The object was accomplished without touching the proper sovereignty of the separate riparian States over the waters within their limits, beyond the necessary restrictions on their right to impose separate duties and burthens on the objects or instruments of commerce. Each State for its own sake would keep the channel of commerce open and free within its own dominions, while making such erections therein as the interests of its own people demanded. That was left to the sovereignty and judgment of the State.

I do not say that a State has any rightful authority to shut up a river, of any considerable importance to the commerce of the country, by physical obstructions, even when exclusively within its own territory, if it runs to the sea. Unimportant streams or creeks may be thus closed for sufficient reasons of police or public policy. It would be a matter between the State and its own people. But in regard to rivers that are really important to commerce, I believe the country might exist under the Constitution for a thousand years, and no such case ever occur. It is quite impossible to suppose, on any reasoning applied to what we know of human conduct, that any such case should occur, so long as the States of the Union remain this side of revolution and open war.

In the case of a river which traverses or separates two or more States, and goes to the sea, I hold it to be equally improbable, and impossible, that the navigation should be closed by any one of the States. There is no conceivable ground of interest, or commercial policy, which should lead the State, holding the mouth of such a river, to shut up the navigation against the States above. Connecticut cannot now stop the produce of Massachusetts, Vermont and New Hampshire, descending the common river between them, at the north line of the State, or at the mouth of the river, and demand duties upon such produce, or send up its own produce or merchandize burthened with State taxes, for the consumers above to pay. It is the very freedom of commerce on such rivers, made thus free by the Constitution and laws of Congress, and with which no State can interfere, that perfectly secures the freedom of navigation upon them, without taking from the States their sovereignty and jurisdiction over them, so necessary to the proper exercise of their powers of local government and police, and to those public improvements which are indispensable to their prosperity.

But if it be thought possible that a State next to the sea, on any ground of interest, or even in a spirit of hostility or injury to a State above, on a river common to them both, should close the navigation between itself and the State above, I suppose it would not be a case altogether beyond judicial cognizance and redress. Imagine the Connecticut river closed by a dam at the boundary between Connecticut and Massachusetts. Here would be "a controversy between two or more States"—a case to which the judicial power of the United States extends, with original jurisdiction in the Supreme Court.

It is not doubted that this jurisdiction was given mainly with reference to disputed boundaries, or titles, between States. But the power is general, and may be applied to a controversy between States in respect to a right of navigation in a common river, as well as to a question of boundary. In questions of boundary, the Court takes cognizance of the cases on the express authority of the Constitution, and decides them upon the laws and usages of nations in disputes of that kind. (Opinion of Ch. J. Taney, in Wheeling Bridge case, 19 Curtis, p. 647.) A controversy between States in regard to the right of navigation on a common river, would also stand on the laws and usages of nations.

And in such a case, I suppose the right of the injured State would be clear. The United States have always maintained that the right of navigation on a river traversing, or separating, several independent States, and running to the sea, was a natural right in all such States, and was so held by the laws of nations. The States above have a right to an open passage to the sea, subject only to the authority of the States below to guard themselves against injury or serious danger. That was the right always maintained by the United States to the free navigation of the Mississippi while Spain held the mouth of that river. And they have earnestly contended for the same right of free navigation on the St. Lawrence. If that is an American doctrine of international law as applicable to independent nations, much more is it applicable to the States of this Union, where the Constitution makes all commerce between them free, and thus greatly strengthens the obligation upon such of them as are below on common rivers, to keep the navigation of such rivers open and free to those States above which have a right to use them, even by the laws and usages of nations.

But, for myself, I do not hold it to be a supposable case that any such violation of the rights of navigation can ever occur, so long as the peace of the Union shall be preserved. The States must go far beyond the line of innocent rivalries under the Constitution—they must become hostile States, and enemies, before they can enter upon measures which can have no object but to see which can do the other most harm. An invasion of one State by the forces of another might as properly be anticipated. If the time should ever arrive when States of this Union shall come into collision, and madly indulge in acts of mutual hostility, it will be time enough then to consider how far the power of the general government may be employed, and in what form, under the Constitution, to meet the difficulty. Failing that, the conflicting and warring sovereignties of the country must be left to find, or make, an issue of peace for themselves, if they can, in their own way. When wars come to be flagrant, laws will of course be silent.

It is not necessary that I should say a word to this Court of the great importance of this principal question of power as between the National and State governments, on which I have now offered my views. If it belongs to the National Government, it is a power which, if once entered upon, has no assignable limit. It is impossible to say where it would end. Certainly, the power being conceded, if we could suppose it possible it should ever be exercised to the full extent to which it might be carried, if once begun, it would leave the States little more than the shadow, and not a great deal of the substance, of sovereignty. Especially would they be stripped of power for some of the highest and most beneficent purposes of government, as thus far employed by them. Those works of public improvement which have been so extensively and happily prosecuted, and which are still carried forward, by the separate States of this Union, or under their authority, and which together constitute a connected system of vast extent and magnitude, and of incalculable value and importance to the nation, and which the National Government never would, and never could have prosecuted as they have been prosecuted by the States, or under their guardianship and power; how much of all these works, these noble signs and instruments of civilization and progress all over the country, would have existed to-day, if Congress had undertaken to press the commercial power conferred upon it, both on the land and on the water, to any thing like the dangerous extent to which it might certainly have been carried, if once entered upon, and acquiesced in? Nobody can say that the attempt would not have been most disastrous.

Fortunately, as I venture to think, and as I have endeavored to convince the Court, Congress does not possess this power over the highways of general commerce, so that in whatsoever might affect their condition and availability for the uses of commerce, the General Government might, if it would, command as sovereign over them all, to the exclusion of the States. Happily, too, as I venture to think, and as I have endeavored to convince the Court, if Congress does possess this power, it has never exercised it. Certainly, as it seems to me, it has wholly refrained, by a settled and unbroken policy, from any attempt to push the commercial power to the extent of controlling, in any degree whatever, State legislation over the navigable waters within State limits, in respect to any works of public improvement in or over them, which a State might think the public interests demanded at its hands. If such has been the policy of Congress, from which it has not departed by any Act of legislation whatever, this Court, I am sure, if so convinced, will be quite satisfied and content not itself to disturb that policy, even if it had the power to disturb it.

With a country already so expanded as ours has become since the Constitution was framed, and destined, perhaps, to embrace still other and more distant regions and peoples, the problem of maintaining such a frame of National Government as the Constitution establishes, in necessary vigor, and, at the same time, in harmony with the separate political Communities which make up the Union, multiplied and multiplying as these separate Communities are, is one which no patriot mind, whether of jurist or statesman, can contemplate without the profoundest anxiety. No thinking man, I imagine, can be found at the present day, who supposes that our Federal system could be maintained at all, but for that ample measure of sovereignty for local government which the Constitution so happily leaves in the hands of the States. Every one, I suppose, now sees that any further weakening of the States, to add strength to the National Government, would have been fatal. The security of the system rests in the fact that every State is, and feels that it is, a real sovereignty and a real government, endowed with original powers, for all that most intimately concerns the welfare and happiness of the people of such State, and is not a mere municipal Corporation with a modicum of authority borrowed from an imperial Power to which it owes its existence.

Nothing, in my judgment, could be more entirely fatal to our system than any disturbance, at the present day, by Constitutional interpretations, of the nicely adjusted balance of powers between the National and State Governments, as fixed by the Constitution. Both must have their own, and nothing which is not their own. And it must needs be remembered that the prerogative of the National Government, which makes it the interpreter and final adjudicator of its own powers, while it is an indispensable, is yet a fearful authority. It is not in the nature of any government voluntarily to abdicate or repudiate any of its just powers. Happy, thrice happy, if the General Government, marching up fully to this line, shall take care not to pass it by so much as the breadth of a hair. But what moderation, what forbearance, what lofty justice, what noble virtue, does not all this demand! And it is this Court to which the country must look as the grand exemplar of these high attributes.

This Court occupies a position of higher dignity, and of more awful responsibility, than attaches, or ever attached, to any other Judicial Tribunal on earth. While it cannot lift a finger of authority, except to administer the law of the land as between litigant parties immediately before it, precisely in the manner of the humblest tribunal of justice, yet, such is the nature of the jurisdiction it is sometimes called upon to exercise, the governments of the country, State and National, the States themselves, and the United States, are, at times, in effect, summoned into its august presence, and dismissed with its authoritative decrees resting upon them. Sublime as this power is, it is not greater than necessity demands; and on its strict preservation depends, in my honest judgment, the issue of the great experiment we are making in the Science of Government. But how is this tremendous power to be preserved, so that it may commend itself to the continued and unabated reverence, submission and obedience of the country? To this question there can be but one answer. While maintaining, with a courage that must never falter, all the just powers of the Government of which it forms an integral department, and all its own just powers, its very existence is staked upon the careful and scrupulous abnegation of all unaccorded or doubtful authority, whether in itself, or in the government of which it forms a part.

www.ingramcontent.com/pod-product-compliance
Lightning Source LLC
Chambersburg PA
CBHW021949160426
43195CB00011B/1296